Foundations
FOR LEARNING

Laurie L. Hazard
BRYANT UNIVERSITY
SMITHFIELD, RHODE ISLAND

Jean-Paul Nadeau
BRISTOL COMMUNITY COLLEGE
FALL RIVER, MASSACHUSETTS

PEARSON

Prentice
Hall

Upper Saddle River, New Jersey
Columbus, Ohio

Library of Congress Cataloging-in-Publication Data

Hazard, Laurie L.
    Foundations for learning/Laurie L. Hazard, Jean-Paul Nadeau.
        p.   cm.
    Includes bibliographical references and index.
        ISBN 0-13-119953-6
    1. Study skills,   2. Learning, Psychology of.   3. Academic achievement.   4. College student
        orientation. I. Nadeau, Jean-Paul.   II. Title.

LB2395.H394 2006
378.1'70281—dc22

                                                                        2005004442

Vice President and Publisher: Jeffery W. Johnston
Executive Editor: Sande Johnson
Editorial Assistant: Susan Kauffman
Production Editor: Holcomb Hathaway
Design Coordinator: Diane C. Lorenzo
Cover Designer: Jeff Vanik
Cover Image: Corbis
Production Manager: Susan Hannahs
Director of Marketing: Ann Castel Davis
Marketing Manager: Amy Judd
Compositor: Integra–Pondicherry, India
Cover Printer: Courier Stoughton, Inc.
Printer/Binder: Courier Stoughton, Inc.

Pearson Education Ltd.   Pearson Education Australia Pty. Limited
Pearson Education Singapore Pte. Ltd.   Pearson Education North Asia Ltd.
Pearson Education Canada, Ltd.   Pearson Educación de Mexico, S.A. de C.V.
Pearson Education Japan   Pearson Education Malaysia Pte. Ltd.

10 9 8 7 6 5 4 3
ISBN 0-13-119953-6

Dedication

To our children, Grace, John, Andrew, and Alison,
whose giggles and smiles at the end of the day
helped sustain the momentum to "keep on going" with this project.

BRIEF CONTENTS

CONTENTS

CHAPTER ONE | ## Claiming Your Education   *1*

CHAPTER TWO | ## Developing Academic Self-Concept   *15*

CHAPTER THREE | ## Planning and Prioritizing   *29*

CHAPTER FOUR
Developing Metacognitive Skills   *51*

CHAPTER FIVE
Developing Communication Skills   *79*

Combining Readings and Notes for Optimal Performance in Lectures and on Exams   105

CHAPTER SIX

A s a first-year student, I found college to be an environment that was so overwhelming that it was almost impossible to stay focused on the reason why I was there in the first place: to earn a degree. How was I expected to handle the substantial workload assigned outside the classroom when I was given the freedom to do whatever I wanted whenever I wanted? As a traditional 18-year-old student, my parents were no longer around to look over my shoulder to make sure that I was doing my homework; it was solely up to me to take part actively in my education.

The pursuit of a college education was a conscious choice I made to improve myself in areas that stretched far beyond the classroom. By the end of the first week of classes, it became quite clear that I could not be successful by just "being there." I had to claim my education as my own. A great deal of responsibility comes with the privilege of having the opportunity to earn a college degree. Maintaining a healthy social environment, practicing time management and effective study skills, and preparing for the tasks assigned were "must dos" for me and anyone else who expected to claim their education and achieve their goals. To build a solid college experience and eventual professional career, I needed a base upon which to build.

The one thing that helped prepare me was a class all first-year students were enrolled in called "Foundations for Learning." The required class was geared specifically toward the issues that all students face. The course was designed in a way that readied me for challenges I would encounter throughout my first year. For example, Chapter One of *Foundations for Learning* helped me to figure out what my school was all about, by describing the inner workings of a collegiate institution and what professors expect of their students.

I thought I knew it all in high school, but college was very different, with much higher expectations. *Foundations for Learning* not only explained to me what it meant to be a college student, but it also taught me the necessary skills I needed to be a successful individual. I learned in Chapter Two that surrounding myself with the right friends who shared the same interests and supported me as an individual was one of the most important decisions I would ever make. With guidance in creating the right social environment, I was now ready to focus on achieving my goals.

The remaining chapters in the textbook helped me understand how I personally learn best and gave me specific strategies for taking different types of tests, writing papers, taking notes, and, most important, managing my time. By learning how to manage my time effectively, through a structured schedule, I found I had ample time to get all my work done, spend time with my friends, and participate in on-campus activities. This has made my college experience both enjoyable and increasingly productive. As a junior, I still hit bumps in the road, whether it is preparing for a complex presentation in my Investments class or finding an effective way to read through a difficult novel in Philosophy. At first I thought the book used in "Foundations for Learning" was just a textbook, but I realize now that I can use it throughout college as a reference for working through problems that I will face in the future.

As I read this book, I realized that it actually works. The principles and skills that I learned and implemented as a result have guided me toward earning an exceptional GPA thus far. By accepting the fact that I did not know everything about school, I was able to acquire effective tools to improve my life as a whole. More than a textbook, *Foundations for Learning* provides guidance on what is necessary to be successful beyond college. It provided me with the tools to take my college experience to the highest level. I believe that the good habits I have developed will undoubtedly transcend into my career in the future. It is now up to you to claim your education.

—*Daniel J. Fiandaca,*
Student Reviewer

Many parents and students all over the globe believe in the value, the usefulness, of earning a college degree. Students believe that earning a college degree will help prepare them for a future career, and parents hope that a college diploma will secure better lives for their children (Boyer, 1987). But a college education means more than salary, status, or security; it means learning about yourself and the communities around you.

Most students believe college will help them become educated and trained for a career, and they think the chief benefit of a college education is its effect on earning power (Levine, 1989). This textbook, *Foundations for Learning*, challenges you to examine other ways that your education will benefit you beyond considering your potential gross income.

A key concept explored in the chapters that follow is making personal choices. One important choice that students often forget they have made is the decision to attend college. The bases for this decision differ from student to student. As one first-year student explains: "I am in college so I can further my education, and get a better job so I can better myself in the long run. I don't always like being here, but I know I have to go to school somewhere. I mean, it's just, what do you have if you don't have an education? You don't really have much."

Another student says: "My mom went to the University of North Carolina, Chapel Hill. She had the same college experience I'm going to have. I see my mom is successful, and I think, I'll do the same thing. I'll be successful." As you read this textbook, think about your decision-making process: why did you decide to attend college, and what do you hope to get out of the experience?

The central philosophy of *Foundations for Learning* is that of "claiming an education," the idea that learning in college demands that students engage with the material presented (Rich, 1977). Although your perception of college may be that you'll sit quietly, taking notes lecture after lecture, you will likely find college to be quite different from your initial expectations. Instead of thinking about college as a place where professors dump information into you that you then "know," *Foundations for Learning* helps you to see that learning is more than mere collection and absorption—and more than doing the minimum amount of work required. Learning involves making connections, taking calculated risks, and being open to change, and these concepts are discussed in the context of your new environment. This textbook helps you to better prepare for learning in a new environment, as well as for the challenges presented by college or university professors.

You'll be encouraged to claim your education in many ways, including working to gain membership in a scholarly community, reflecting on your academic self-concept, developing your planning abilities, becoming more aware of the ways in which you think and learn, communicating more effectively in writing and in class discussion, and approaching classes and exams in a manner that enables deep processing as opposed to rote memorization. These topics are presented in the context of current research as well as the voices of first-year students, whose experiences are highlighted in narratives and "student portrait" boxes in each chapter.

Two other concepts stressed repeatedly across chapters are the ideas of being open to change and being able to self-reflect. As you'll read in Chapter One, the transition from a high school to a college environment means rethinking your attitudes and behaviors related to learning. As you make this transition, you will be most successful if you are able to reflect periodically upon these attitudes and behaviors—*and* if you have the motivation, and, it is hoped, the humility, you will be able to work toward making any necessary changes. If, for example, you understand the theory surrounding breaking down large assignments into manageable pieces but don't ever put the theory into practice, you won't benefit.

Institutions of higher education recognize that there is a need to support students as they face the increasing academic demands of college. First-year experience courses, academic success centers, academic advising, tutoring services, writing centers, and other student-centered initiatives are the avenues through which they provide this support. Discussing effective ways to maximize first-year students' capabilities for academic success—indeed, how to get the most out of the aforementioned opportunities—is the primary goal of *Foundations for Learning*. This text focuses on the process of learning how to learn, developing academic performance techniques, and cultivating the habits of mind for lifelong achievement and success.

Chapter One helps you to clarify your responsibilities as a college student and what professors and college/university staff expect of you both in and out of the classroom. You will find at the college level that you will be asked to take a significantly more active role in your own learning than you did in high school. In the college environment, if you choose not to do the reading in chemistry, for example, your teacher won't make you stay after school; instead, you won't be able to contribute to the class discussion, will have to squeeze in this reading at a later date, and will feel like you have fallen behind. On the other hand, if you choose to read an unassigned text about a subject mentioned briefly in your Western civilization class, you won't necessarily be given special recognition or "credit." Discovering and exploring your interests is what college is all about.

Chapter One asks you to clarify your responsibilities as a college student and to think about how you will handle meeting the heightened academic expectations of higher education. Chapter Two helps you to conduct a more in-depth exploration of what Chapter One asks you to do. Chapter Two asks you to reflect on your thoughts and feelings about your continuing role as a student and how those thoughts and feelings may influence your ability to meet the many demands you will be facing. Further, Chapter Two challenges you to explore your relationships with your family, your peers, and your new relationship with your college or university, and how these relationships will contribute to your role as a student.

Chapter Three centers on prioritizing your time as a college student. Eleanor Roosevelt once said, "If you want something done, ask a busy person," implying that people who have a lot to do, and get it all done, must be highly organized. Procrastination, the enemy of those of us who need to manage our time systematically, is also addressed.

In Chapter Four, the focus shifts to metacognitive strategies. Metacognition literally means "thinking about how you think." Here, you will read about strategies that help you learn about how you think: by using writing, namely, writing to learn and journal writing, as well as reading, including a technique called "text annotation." Chapter Five covers developing communication skills with a focus on college-level writing. Writing the research paper is another activity introduced in this chapter, including suggestions regarding how to select a topic, how to gather useful information, and how to cite sources properly. Other important communication skills are discussed here as well, including becoming a participant in class discussions and making effective in-class presentations.

In an effort to help you get more out of studying than the ability to recall information for a 24-hour period, Chapter Six explores numerous active reading, note-taking, and study methods that will help you benefit from what you have learned long into the future. These methods include how you read a textbook before you go to class, listen and take notes during lectures, and review your notes and readings after you've attended a lecture. You'll also see the importance of synthesizing the notes you've taken in class with the material from your readings. Of course, students often prefer to study in groups, and Chapter Six also explains how to conduct productive study group sessions. Finally, Chapter Six outlines a step-by-step process for responding to various types of exam questions.

Foundations for Learning, then, offers insight into how to be a successful college student so that you don't have to learn everything the hard way. If you read this textbook with an open mind and are willing to implement the many strategies, suggestions, and pieces of advice offered, you are likely to discover new ways to engage with peers and course material. In other words, you will more easily adapt to your new environment. You will also be reminded of what is expected of college students—and the importance of your attitude toward your own education. As you turn these pages, read actively, be willing to change, and begin your journey toward membership in a community of learners.

REFERENCES

Boyer, E. (1987). *College: The undergraduate experience in America.* New York: Harper & Row.

Levine, A. (1989). *Shaping higher education's future: Demographic realities and opportunities 1990–2000.* San Francisco: Jossey-Bass.

Rich, A. (1977). *Claiming an education.* Speech delivered to the students of Douglas College, Rutgers University, New Brunswick, New Jersey.

CHAPTER ONE

Claiming Your Education

BECOMING PART OF A SCHOLARLY COMMUNITY

Much has taken place at your college or university before your arrival on campus. Students have been working on case studies, conducting chemistry experiments, composing book-length master's theses, and having discussions about Foucault over coffee. Residence hall directors have developed a growing understanding of the needs of students, and food services has worked on providing a diverse and healthy menu for students. The director of the library has been continually updating the library's print and on-line offerings, and the information technology department has worked to ensure that classroom labs are equipped with the latest technology. Students from across the country and all over the globe have traveled the same sidewalks and traversed the same corridors you now do.

So how will you react to this bustling campus and its ongoing conversations? This textbook encourages you to be an active participant in this dialogue; you've walked into an enormous room full of people talking—listen for a while if you would like, but don't forget to offer your own contributions. Rhetorician Kenneth Burke's (1973) explanation of this concept has been referred to as the Burkean parlor:

> Imagine that you enter a parlor. You come late. When you arrive, others have long preceded you, and they are engaged in a heated discussion, a discussion too heated for them to pause and tell you exactly what it is about. In fact, the discussion had already begun long before any of them got there, so that no one present is qualified to retrace for you all the steps that had gone before. You listen for a while, until you decide that you have caught the tenor of the argument; then you put in your oar. Someone answers; you answer him; another comes to your defense; another aligns himself against you, to either the embarrassment or gratification of your opponent, depending upon the quality of your ally's assistance. However, the discussion is interminable. The hour grows late, you must depart. And you do depart, with the discussion still vigorously in progress. (pp. 110–111)

IN THIS CHAPTER

- Do you possess intellectual curiosity?
- What do your professors expect of you?
- What are your responsibilities as a member of the campus community?
- What role do you play in the learning process?
- How does working with others result in scholarship?
- What is meant by academic honesty, plagiarism, and intellectual property?

Make It Personal

How will you react to your bustling campus and its ongoing conversations?

1

In *Foundations for Learning,* you will enter into an ongoing discussion regarding the factors that lead to college success. You will hear what experts in the field have to say regarding the philosophies and techniques addressed; in effect, you will be provided with a rationale for the advice offered. This research stretches back over 30 years in some cases, and it is important to consider the history regarding these concepts in order to apply them to current situations—your college education, say—in an educated way.

As a college or university student, then, you have the opportunity to join a **scholarly community**, a group of people working toward intellectual pursuits, but your membership is not guaranteed. You must work toward familiarizing yourself with the guiding principles of that community and aspire toward them if you are to be considered a peer.

You may be asking yourself, "Besides fellow classmates, who are my peers in this environment?" The answer may surprise you. Professors are experts in their respective fields—or scholarly communities—who are helping students gain access to, and membership in, these same communities. In the context of the classroom, for example, students are expected to engage in scholarly discussions with their professors; raise questions; and, at times, even challenge them.

> ### Student Portrait
>
> **Kay:** "I can't really talk to my professors. It's because they're kind of evaluating you, and so like you go on a more personal basis with them. I don't feel very comfortable about it. My science teacher right now, I don't feel too comfortable around him 'cause I'm not doing too great in his class. It's like they're up there, and you're all the way down here. That's how it is to me."

For a moment, think about your professors' perspective. From their vantage point, you have made a life-altering decision to attend college. As an adult, in control of your own destiny, you have chosen to enter into a scholarly community and work toward earning membership. This process is very different from attending high school, which is a compulsory endeavor. The assumption here is that college is a carefully arrived at, well-thought-out choice. You *want* to be in college. You are excited about, and interested in, many, if not most, of the topics presented to you, and you are highly motivated to master new bodies of knowledge.

You'll make many more choices now that you are attending college. You will also, for example, need to decide which courses you'd like to take, and the professor and student contract is one way you demonstrate your willingness to engage with the material in each of those courses.

THE PROFESSOR AND STUDENT CONTRACT

Teaching and learning are enhanced when teachers and learners have shared expectations regarding course outcomes. For this reason, college professors construct a **syllabus**, a document outlining the desired course outcomes and other relevant information for each course they teach. Syllabi are usually shared with students during the first week of class, if not the first day or earlier.

Each syllabus you are given will help you understand important information about the course and your professor: what goals you are expected to strive toward, what will be expected of you, how your work will be assessed, and perhaps even what a typical class meeting might involve.

It would be beneficial, then, to consider each syllabus carefully, understanding that your acceptance of the professor's terms—even if this is conveyed through silent approval—is a prerequisite for remaining a student in that class. If you have questions about what you should expect after reading the syllabus, ask your professor. Conscious acceptance of, and continued adherence to, your course contract is part of being a responsible member of a scholarly community.

Conscious acceptance of, and continued adherence to, your course contract is part of being a responsible member of a scholarly community.

Keep your syllabi handy throughout the semester. These documents often include a listing of topics, assignments, and other such information you'll need to know in order to be prepared for future class meetings. Your professor may very well include a list of all of your assignments on the course syllabus and not mention them again until they are collected for grading. This information can be quite useful when you are planning your schedule in an attempt to manage your time effectively and efficiently. We'll talk more about this in Chapter Three.

The key is to remember that the syllabus is an essential component of being a responsible member of a scholarly community. **Responsibility** literally means your response-ability, that is, your ability to choose a response. Ultimately, how you choose to respond to the requirements of your syllabi, for instance, will dictate your academic experience. Will you embrace all of the suggested assignments and complete them to the best of your ability or will you respond by skipping books on your supplemental reading list? As you will soon learn, the level at which you adhere to your syllabus has implications for how much you will learn each semester.

One last bit of advice regarding course syllabi: many times your syllabi will include guiding questions to focus your attention on certain topics or themes in a course. Pay close attention to such questions, for it would not be unusual to see them again in some form on a test or exam. The process of using the syllabus to predict test and exam questions is covered in more detail in Chapter Six. For now, know that it will be primarily up to you to determine, based on the delivery of course material, what questions will appear on a test or exam. To do so with reliability, you must be actively engaged with your professors in **intellectual discourse**, in other words, the ability to have a rational discussion about a particular subject with interested others. This type of conversation will necessitate asking questions and searching for answers, which will ultimately lead to more questions. As in the Burkean parlor, the idea is that the conversation does not end when you leave the (class) room. To experience such discourse, though, requires that teachers and learners alike possess the trait of intellectual curiosity.

INTELLECTUAL CURIOSITY

You may need to self-reflect to determine whether you possess intellectual curiosity. Peggy Maki (2002), an expert in higher education assessment, defines **intellectual curiosity** as "the characteristic ability to question, challenge, look at an issue from multiple perspectives, seek more information before rushing to judgment, raise questions, deliberate, and craft well-reasoned arguments" (p. 6). You may use what you have read so far in this chapter to help you determine whether you do, in fact, possess a high degree of intellectual curiosity.

Start out by asking yourself, "If I come across something I don't know or don't understand, what do I normally do? Do I skip the concept and hope the professor will deliver the answer in the next class?" For instance, in the first paragraph of this chapter, when you encountered the last name of an individual, Foucault, did you attempt to investigate who this person was if you did not already know? If you did, you may have discovered that he was a French philosopher and social critic who himself possessed intellectual curiosity. As he reflects on why he was attracted to a scholarly environment, he muses:

> **Make It Personal**
>
> If you come across something you don't know or don't understand, what do you normally do?

We did not know when I was ten or eleven years old, whether we would become German or remain French. We would not know whether we would die or not in the bombing, and so on. When I was sixteen or seventeen I knew only one thing: school life was an environment protected from exterior menaces, politics. And I have always been fascinated by living in a protected scholarly environment, in an intellectual milieu. Knowledge is for me that which must function as a protection of individual existence and as a comprehension of the exterior world. I think that's it. Knowledge as a means of surviving by understanding. (quoted in Foss, Foss, & Trapp, 1991, p. 210)

If you possess intellectual curiosity, you might read these statements and, if it's not immediately apparent, assume that the reference in the first few sentences is to World War II. If you were not sure, you might investigate further. You might read this passage and wonder what it would be like for a 10- or 11-year-old to face his or her mortality, question Foucault's perspective that school life is protected from exterior menaces and perhaps disagree with this assertion, consider what knowledge means to Foucault and thereby reflect on your own definition of knowledge, or wonder what he means when he says that knowledge is a means of "surviving by understanding."

Indeed, an intellectually curious individual collects and processes information in an elaborate, sophisticated manner. This manner of thinking is a habit, a disposition; the intellectually curious individual is in a routine of thinking deeply. You may be concerned that when you read Foucault's passage you did not "wonder" to the extent that was described. Perhaps you did not wonder at all. You may be feeling anxious that you do not possess a disposition toward intellectual curiosity and, without this, cannot earn membership into a scholarly community.

Fortunately, like training your body to run a marathon, you can train your mind toward the disposition of intellectual curiosity. To do so requires a particular mind-set; it requires you to be *active*. You need to begin by analyzing ways in which you learn, and start thinking about how you are going to approach the endeavor of joining a scholarly community.

ACTIVE VS. PASSIVE LEARNING

The distinction that will be made here between activity and passivity does not have to do with physical behaviors, but with psychological mind-sets. One of these mind-sets is that of the passive learner. **Passive learners,** whether consciously or unconsciously subscribing to the philosophy of passivity, expect faculty to teach them what they need to know (and *only* what they need to know). They want the library to have the journal article or book they need when they need it, and they wouldn't consider reading an essay or book that was not required reading in one of their classes. They glance through assigned material with minimal investment, expecting that the professor will offer a clear and concise summary and analysis of the reading. They may even expect the professor to tell them exactly what questions will appear on an upcoming test. After all, goes the thinking, why are they paying all of that money for tuition, anyway?

A philosophy more beneficial to college students is that of the active learner. **Active learners** believe that students are not at college to be acted upon and led through a series of disjointed activities toward some fuzzy end indicated by the receipt of a diploma. Active learning is about students becoming agents in their own educational process. After all, who has a greater stake in this process than the student learner?

Active learning is about students becoming agents in their own educational process.

Active learning involves doing many of the things suggested in this textbook. Take reading, for example, or, more precisely, *active* reading. Instead of passively highlighting most of a chapter with only a moderate level of comprehension, active readers engage more directly with the text. Some active readers perform text annotation, a technique we discuss in Chapter Four, whereby the student's reaction to what is read is noted in the margins of the text itself. In this manner, questions can be asked—questions to which the student sincerely seeks answers. These questions could be brought up in class or during faculty office hours.

The ardent active learner likely wouldn't wait until class to seek out answers, however. The active learner's intellectual curiosity would encourage her to search for answers to her questions: in the index of the text in question, in other works that the author has written, in works by other authors on the same subject. The goal of an active learner is to come to a better understanding, the consequence of which is asking more questions and searching for more answers.

Similarly, active listening requires you to carefully consider what a speaker has to say. An active listener identifies a speaker's main idea as well as the rationale used to support that idea. Equally important is what may be lacking from the speaker's rationale. Rest assured, for example, that members of Congress, particularly those aligned with the opposing political party, will listen actively to the president's State of the Union Address. They are interested in the President's focus: what topics have been emphasized, and which have been de-emphasized or avoided entirely? They are interested in the reasoning and evidence employed by the President. Oftentimes the State of the Union Address is followed by criticism made by members of the opposing party, criticism resulting from active listening. Active listening, then, as does active reading, leads to questions.

Even the most active of learners will, at times, get stuck in their quest for answers. They may, at these moments, resist thinking about a problem in different ways, a concept that two psychologists, Friedman and Lipshitz (1992), termed **automatic thinking**. Automatic thinking is efficient when dealing with routine activities and situations such as getting dressed. Yet, as Friedman and Lipshitz note, the advantage of automatic thinking can become a disadvantage when in the face of change or uncertainty. They argue that automatic thinking leads people to rely on what they already know; it contributes to a tendency to ignore critical information and rely on standard behavior repertoires when change is required. That is, people will continue to do what they feel most comfortable doing even if it isn't working for them. They resist change.

Make It Personal
How might automatic thinking affect you as a first-year student?

Accepting the assertion that automatic thinking can be a disadvantage when in the face of change or uncertainty, how do you think automatic thinking might affect you as a first-year student? One of the major changes you will confront as a first-year student is uncertainty in approaching studying for your college courses. You will likely find out that the study skills you utilized in high school will not produce the same results when you apply them to college-level courses. Practitioners who help first-year students develop college-level study habits report that, indeed, students tend to cling to their old, comfortable habits even if these habits don't produce the hoped for results.

Consider a first-year student, Colleen, who completed high school with a B+ average. For her first major college exam, Colleen does what she did in high school—waits until the night before to study. She diligently begins to prepare index cards, recording an important definition on each card. She finds that with the large volume of information she needs to know, it is taking her a lot longer to make index cards than it ever did before. "That's okay," she says to herself, "I'm in college now; this *should* take a little longer." After four hours of making index cards, it is well past midnight. Poor Colleen has run out of time and is too exhausted to review the cards that she has made. She's a little nervous but reasons that she has spent twice as much time studying than she had ever done before, so she should be ready. She takes the exam. It's much more difficult than she expected, and she is confused by some of the questions. She earns a C on her first college-level exam.

This mediocre grade is a bit of a blow to Colleen's ego. After all, in her estimation, she is not a C student; she's at least a B student. In her view, this grade is a failure. She reflects on the experience in earnest and grants that she did wait too long to prepare her index cards, leaving her no time to review. The next test comes along three weeks later and she sets about making her index cards well in advance, this time leaving ample time for review. At the end of her grueling, eight-hour study session, she has each and every index card memorized backward and forward. She is ready for the test! In fact, she's energized and excited; she feels in total control of the material. Never has she been so dedicated to her studies. This amount of effort should surely yield an A. But her exam is returned with a grade of 76 marked clearly at the top, another C.

How could this happen? She worked so hard. She put in what she considered an inordinate amount of effort. For Colleen, studying for eight hours was unprecedented. This time, she feels angry, frustrated, and helpless. She did exactly what she was supposed to do! In her automatic-thinking mode, she never considered that the grade might have resulted from *how* she was studying. Although she adjusted the length of time spent studying, her two approaches were identical. With automatic thinking, people tend to see only what they know and ignore critical information. When it comes to change, they gravitate toward their comfort zone. Colleen never considered that making index cards or relying on memorization as a learning skill was what wasn't working. She automatically assumed that her personal failure resulted from the *time* she spent studying.

The negative consequences of automatic thinking can contribute to failure. Active thinking, argue Friedman and Lipshitz (1992), "enables people to see situations differently and to experiment with novel responses. It also enables them to become aware of how they select, interpret, and act on information about themselves and the contexts in which they act" (p. 119). Someone once said that the definition of insanity is doing the same thing over and over again and expecting different results. Becoming an active learner requires a student to experiment with new ways of learning, particularly if his or her old ways aren't yielding the desired results.

Changing requires a certain amount of risk taking. Changing from automatic thinking to active thinking is not easy; it requires students to take full responsibility for their own learning. That is not to say that a student will have to attempt to "**switch cognitive gears**," or go from one mode of thought to another, alone (Louis & Sutton, 1991, p. 119). On a college campus, there are many people who can help.

The faculty and staff of institutions of higher education want students to be successful. For this reason, these individuals establish mechanisms by which students can bolster their understanding of course material outside of the classroom. Some of these mechanisms are faculty office hours, tutoring and writing centers, counseling centers, and language labs, all integral parts of the scholarly community. The prevailing thought on a college campus is that learning occurs both inside and outside the classroom. To get the most out of your college experience, you must expect that all students will engage in extensive out-of-classroom learning.

You may be required to utilize and/or familiarize yourself with some of the aforementioned academic programs and services. More than likely, however, you will have quite a bit of choice as to when, how frequently, and for what purposes you do so. If, for example, your economics professor requires students to visit the tutoring center "periodically" during the course of the semester, it is up to students to decide what "periodically" will mean for them. For some, periodically might mean visiting the center the day before each exam to work with a tutor to make sure they comprehend the material that they've studied. For others, periodically might mean a weekly appointment to review class materials to prevent the possibility of getting "lost." Although the choice is up to you, it is strongly suggested that you consciously consider the way(s) you plan on using each service—in other words, to take response-ability, to be an active learner, and to claim these services as part of your education—and that you realize that the way you use a resource will affect what you get out of the experience.

Many times students' attitudes prevent them from seeking help. Some students who end up in academic difficulty at the end of the semester confess that they were just too proud or embarrassed to ask for help. For some, the inability to ask for help may result in poor grades. In a scholarly community, the expectation is that you will be an active learner, that you will search for clarification using all available resources. If you use the study techniques suggested in this textbook and talk with your professor during office hours, you are doing some of the right things. You should also utilize tutoring services offered at your institution. Tutoring isn't a quick fix; it involves an ongoing relationship with a fellow student, a student with whom you can have productive dialogues regarding course materials. Tutors can help confirm what you *do* understand as well as help you gain a better understanding of what you *don't*.

COLLABORATION

What better way to join a scholarly community than by working with one or more individuals toward a common goal? You will be afforded many such opportunities, and you should resist any urge you may feel to play it safe, stay in your automatic mode of thinking, and make the collaborative effort an individual one. In other words, don't try to complete a collaborative assignment or task by yourself. You will learn far more if you are forced to consider the opinions of others, assign tasks, track progress, and develop interpersonal communication skills in the process. If collaboration is successful, the work of a group surpasses what would have been possible through the work of a single individual. Andrea Lunsford (2002) admonishes students to debate with group members: "Expect disagreement, and remember that the goal is not for everyone just to 'go along.' The challenge is to get a really spirited debate going and to argue through all possibilities" (p. 34).

"What types of collaborative activities might I participate in?" you ask. These might involve in-class group work, study groups, group presentations, debates, and group papers/projects, to name a few of the more common activities. These situations are unique in their own way; just think about how long you have to get the group dynamic sorted out for in-class group work as opposed to a semester-long group project. Several of these situations are discussed in the chapters that follow.

Through collaboration, you'll learn when and how to make concessions in order to arrive at a final product that is truly the work of an entire group.

Although many students dread collaboration, what they tend to call "group work," you will likely learn much about yourself and others from these experiences. You'll be learning to synthesize ideas—those of your own and those of other individuals both in and outside your group. Through collaboration, you'll learn when and how to make concessions in order to arrive at a final product that is truly the work of an entire group. Eugene Raudsepp (1984) neatly sums up the benefits of collaboration:

Effective teamwork encourages each member to contribute his knowledge to the overall effort. . . . This combination of experience and trading of ideas enables them to learn from each other. It stimulates them to learn more, and to consider a greater variety of variables when solving problems. It brings out most of their latent abilities and provides an atmosphere for continuous growth and development. . . . Cooperative action by each of them contributes to a total effect that is greater than the sum of their independent contributions. (quoted in Beckman, 1990, p. 129)

DOING RESEARCH

A discussion about scholarly communities would not be complete without mentioning **research**. Scholars investigate what others have said and/or written about topics in which they are interested. They use libraries and the Internet to perform some of this investigation. They also use the references in the works they find to lead to other useful sources. In addition to these solitary activities, scholars talk to peers, other scholars in their field—at meetings, at conferences, on the phone, and in person. In these ways, scholars stay up to date regarding their particular interests, whether those include molecular biology or still photography.

The research that is accessed first has to be conducted. In other words, the study that is referenced in Joe's master's thesis initially had to be performed. This aspect of research is another important contribution of scholars, namely adding to the body of knowledge in their particular field. Through new research, scholars hope to say something that hasn't (quite) been said, make connections across/ through ideas, and/or offer an analysis of previous research that helps others view the research in new ways. When making these connections and offering analyses of previous research, scholars write with *academic honesty,* meaning they cite others' work and intellectual efforts.

How do you fit in to all of this? Well, as a scholar-in-the-making, you will be engaging in both of the aforementioned activities. You'll be familiarizing yourself with the body of knowledge in a number of disciplines, and you'll also be making your own contributions to the ongoing conversation. If this seems like an impossible goal, consider that these contributions will likely be small at first, but that all contributions potentially move the discussion forward.

PLAGIARISM AND INTELLECTUAL PROPERTY

O ne topic that professors often bring up when talking to students about an upcoming research project is plagiarism. Have you ever had the experience of someone taking credit for your idea? This act, presenting someone else's ideas as if they were your own, is referred to as **plagiarism**. Plagiarism violates the concept of academic honesty. However, presentation of someone else's ideas is not in and of itself plagiarism. If it were, scholars would be working in isolation, not benefiting from each other's work. Researchers and scholars commonly refer to each other's ideas, giving attribution to the sources of those ideas—whether those

Attribution is the key to avoiding plagiarism.

ideas were discovered through an interview, a newspaper article, a book, a listserv discussion, or a website. Attribution is the key to avoiding plagiarism.

Some institutions subscribe to a service such as Turnitin.com, a website that serves as a clearinghouse for student essays. Professors may request that you submit your essay electronically to this site. Turnitin.com then checks the paper to determine whether the work is original—or whether there is a case of plagiarism.

Whether your paper will undergo electronic scrutiny or that of your professors, you need to be sure that you have credited others for their ideas. Your college or university likely has clearly outlined some rather strict consequences for committing plagiarism in your student handbook. Why is plagiarism considered such a serious offense? The primary reason is likely that producing scholarship—conducting research and publishing findings, say—is hard work that often takes years and, many times, the efforts of multiple individuals. The result of this labor is called **intellectual property**. This property is unique in some way: it contains some new concept or data set or perhaps argues against a previously established correlation. At any rate, it is important that those integrating this intellectual property into their own research acknowledge the efforts of the authors. We'll talk more about plagiarism and the ethics of research in Chapter Five.

CLAIMING AN EDUCATION

T hink back to the concept of responsibility defined earlier in this chapter: the ability to choose a response. You possess the power of choice. You have the ability to choose how you will respond to the new environment of higher education and the opportunities offered at your institution. *Foundations for Learning* urges you to take responsibility for your educational choices and be an active participant in the experience. The foundation for optimal learning experiences at the college level rests in your ability to recognize your role and responsibility as a student. The person who has perhaps encapsulated this idea best is Adrienne Rich, a famous poet. In a convocation speech given in 1977, she implores students to actively claim their education. She explains:

> The first thing I want to say to you who are students is that you cannot afford to think of being here to *receive* an education: you will do much better to think of being here to *claim* one. One of the dictionary definitions of the verb "*to claim*" is: *to take as the rightful owner; to assert in the face of possible contradiction.* "To receive" is *to come into possession of; to act as receptacle or container for; to accept as authoritative or true.* The difference is that between acting and being acted upon. (paragraph 2)

Note the distinction between "acting" and "being acted upon." What Rich is emphasizing here is that you have the choice to act upon the new environment of your institution or you can allow your first year to unfold, merely go with the flow, and simply let your college education happen to you.

Psychologists such as Albert Bandura (1986) and Walter Mischel make similar distinctions. Bandura coined the term **reciprocal determinism**, which identifies the notion that there is a relationship between the person and the environment. Students can certainly be influenced by the new situations they'll find in college, but they can also choose how to behave (Pervin & John, 1977). Mischel (1976) elaborates on the concept of reciprocal determinism in action:

> The image is one of the human being as an active, aware, problem solver, capable of profiting from an enormous range of experiences and cognitive capacities, possessing great potential for good or ill, actively constructing his or her psychological world, and influencing the environment, but also being influenced by it in lawful ways. (quoted in Pervin & John, 1997, p. 404)

If you choose to take sole responsibility for your education and "claim" it, that is, take it as opposed to receive it, the way in which Rich suggests, you will have the capability of profiting from the great range of experiences that await you.

The argument here is that how you interact with this new environment is entirely up to you. It is ultimately your responsibility. You may be wondering what responsibility means relative to learning, and perhaps even living, at your institution. Rich's (1977) convocation speech clearly outlines for students what responsibility means in terms of higher education. What follows are just a few of the ways she describes the concept of responsibility:

- "refusing to let others do your thinking, talking, and naming for you"
- "learning to respect and use your own brains and instincts; hence, grappling with hard work"
- "insisting that those to whom you give your friendship and love are able to respect your mind"
- not "falling for shallow, easy solutions"
- "insisting on a life of meaningful work"
- having "the courage to be different"
- "expecting your faculty to take you seriously"
- "refusing to sell your talents and aspirations short" (paragraphs 7 and 8)

Rich's definition of responsibility acts as great advice for how you might think about conducting yourself during your first year. Which pieces of advice can you see yourself putting into action? Consider the first bit of advice, "refusing to let others do your thinking, talking, and naming for you." You might think, "Well, that depends. Who are the *others*?" The answer is whomever you have well-established relationships with or whomever you decide to enter into relationships with in the future. According to reciprocal determinism, not only will your relationships influence you, but you will also shape others. How relationships influence your academic endeavors is more closely explored in the next chapter.

In this chapter, we have looked at various ways that you can claim your education, both in and out of the classroom, academically and socially. Our hope is that you will stake a more assertive claim and that you will continue to evaluate the extent to which you are driving your educational process.

DISCUSSION QUESTIONS

1. Are you currently a primarily active learner or passive learner? What leads you to draw this conclusion about yourself?
2. What specific actions can you take to gain membership into a scholarly community? What does it mean to be an active participant in one's education?
3. What is the relationship between campus resources and active learning?
4. You've likely received a number of course syllabi fairly recently. What do these documents have in common? Of what importance will these documents be in the remaining weeks of the semester?
5. Did your expectations regarding one or more of your classes change after having read the syllabus? How so or not?
6. Describe the ways in which you have demonstrated intellectual curiosity in the last week or so. Are you satisfied with the extent to which you have done so?
7. When have you engaged in automatic thinking? Why did you do so? What were the consequences?
8. Describe your previous collaborative experiences. Did you find them beneficial? What did you learn? What challenges do you face? Would you do anything differently the next time you collaborate?
9. What specific steps are you taking to claim your education?
10. Define what responsibility means to you. To what extent does Rich's definition of responsibility reflect your own?

ACTIVITIES

1.1 Identify a term or concept you heard or read about this week and use this entry to ask questions to which you seek answers. Ask classmates, professors, staff members, friends, and/or family what they know about the term or concept. Perform a search on the Internet. Search the library's databases. Log your search—as well as your findings—in a journal entry or write an essay.

1.2 After completing the first assignment in one of your classes, visit your professor during office hours. To demonstrate your intellectual curiosity, engage in a conversation about a question you had while completing the reading, what you'd like to accomplish through taking the class, or your professor's current research interests.

1.3 Utilize the services of one of the many campus resources available at your institution (e.g., the campus library or tutoring center). Write a journal entry or short essay about your experience utilizing that resource. What did you expect before you arrived? How did the actual visit correspond to your expectations? Were you satisfied with the outcome? How so or not?

1.4 Over the course of the next week or so, compile a list of terms with which you are not familiar. These terms may come from readings, lectures, class discussion, or TV, for that matter. Then seek out explanations/definitions for these words or phrases. What does this exercise tell you about your education? Are you intellectually curious?

1.5 Research first-year experience (FYE) courses at other institutions. Create a thesis (e.g., FYE courses have grown in number exponentially in the last 10 years, or most FYE courses focus on the same thing—helping students develop college-level study skills) and support your findings with evidence from three sources.

1.6 Examine the policies in place for committing plagiarism at your institution, information that can likely be found in your student handbook. How is plagiarism defined? What are the consequences of such an act? Are you satisfied with the explanation(s) offered?

1.7 Generate a list of your expectations of your professors prior to attending your first classes. Now compare these expectations to your observations after attending classes. What strikes you about this comparison?

1.8 Attend a campus organizational fair. What clubs and/or organizations would you be interested in joining? What would be your motivation for doing so? How would getting involved in this way possibly help you in ways you may not have considered?

1.9 Rich's definition of responsibility acts as great advice for how you might think about conducting yourself during your first year. For each of the eight pieces of advice, describe at least one example of how you might put the advice into action.

REFERENCES

Bandura, A. (1986). *Social foundation of thought and action: A social-cognitive theory*. Englewood Cliffs, NJ: Prentice Hall.

Beckman, M. (1990). Collaborative learning. *College Teaching, 38*(4), 128–133.

Burke, K. (1973). *The philosophy of literary form* (3rd ed.). Berkeley: University of California Press.

Foss, S., Foss, K., & Trapp, R. (1991). *Contemporary perspectives on rhetoric* (2nd ed.). Prospect Heights, IL: Waveland.

Friedman, V. J., & Lipshitz, R. (1992). Teaching people to shift cognitive gears: Overcoming resistance on the road to model II. *Journal of Applied Behavioral Research, 28*(1), 118–136.

Louis, M. R., & Sutton, R. I. (1991). Switching cognitive gears: From habits of mind to active thinking. *Human Relations, 44*(1), 55–76.

Lunsford, A. (2002). *The everyday writer* (2nd ed.). Boston: St. Martin's Press.

Maki, P. (2002). Moving from paperwork to pedagogy: Channeling intellectual curiosity into a commitment to assessment [On-line]. *American Association for Higher Education Bulletin, 54*(9), 3–5.

Pervin, L., & John, O. (1997). *Personality theory and research* (7th ed). New York: John Wiley & Sons.

Rich, A. (1977). *Claiming an education.* Speech delivered to the students of Douglas College, Rutgers University, New Brunswick, New Jersey.

Developing Academic Self-Concept

S elf-concept is a sizable part of your personality. Essentially, **self-concept** encompasses all of our thoughts and feelings (Maslow, 1970). If someone were to ask you, "Who are you?" and you responded by describing some of your thoughts and feelings, you would be providing him or her with some insight into your self-concept. What is of particular interest to personality psychologists is how people develop their self-concept and how it contributes to and organizes their experiences (Pervin & John, 1997). Your self-concept is important to consider because personality psychologists have discovered that our awareness of ourselves influences our experiences and research suggests that how we feel about ourselves affects our behavior in many situations. Well, most of you are experiencing a relatively novel situation: you are new college students. If what personality psychologists have discovered is true, then you may wish to begin to reflect on how you feel about yourself and how those feelings might affect how you will behave as a new college student.

> **IN THIS CHAPTER**
>
> - What kind of student are you?
> - How will your family affect your college experience?
> - How will you relate to your roommate(s) and classmate(s)?
> - What type of relationship will you develop with your institution?

Examining questions such as, "Who am I?" and "How do I feel about myself?" is not as easy a task as it may initially seem. Yet, now that you are in the midst of your first year of college, you may wish to consider these questions seriously. "Who am I and how is my sense of self contributing to and organizing my experiences at college thus far?" Investigating such questions will help you determine how you are likely to relate to this new academic environment. To help you focus your thinking, you may wish to consider specifically, "Who am I as a student and how will that affect my behavior in the wide variety of new situations that I will find myself in while here at college?" In other words, "What is my **academic self-concept?**"

If self-concept encompasses all of your thoughts and feelings, then your academic self-concept would include all of your thoughts and feelings that might affect you as a student. Interior thoughts such as, "I'd rather make friends than strive for a solid A average," "I have never been good at math," or "I do better when I am under pressure," will all affect your performance as a student.

In thinking about your academic self-concept, you will want to start by considering how your academic self-concept developed. For example, what might your **academic autobiography** look like? That is, what type of student were you in elementary school? Middle school? High school? How exactly did your academic self-concept evolve through your years of schooling? How will these early learning experiences shape your academic self-concept in college? As long as you are a student, your academic self-concept will likely continue to develop and, it is hoped, even transform during college.

Reflecting on your past experiences with school is only one of the many ways to think about your developing academic self-concept. Personality psychologists contend that environmental factors such as your family and other close personal relationships influence who you are and how you behave. The environment of your college campus and your living situation, for example, are factors that will affect you as a student. Aside from your "academic autobiography," you should consider how such factors as family and friends influence the type of student you are and how you have been conducting yourself in college.

Essentially, thinking about your family's influence on your academic self-concept is an exercise in thinking about where you've been, your past. Investigating your current close personal relationships will help you figure out what's happening in the here and now, the present.

Your academic self-concept will develop and transform over the course of your college career whether or not you are keenly aware of it. It is a good idea for you to establish an accurate perception of those factors, both positive and negative, that are likely to influence your academic self-concept. Recall Mischel's words and the idea of reciprocal determinism from Chapter One. He explains that we all possess "great potential for good or ill" as we actively influence the environment, but that we are also influenced by the environment and those with whom we choose to form relationships. As you read the rest of this chapter, keep his words and the idea of reciprocity in mind. How will you contribute to the shaping of your relationships and your institution, and how will they, in turn, influence you?

RELATING TO YOUR FAMILY AND CULTURE: HOW YOUR ACADEMIC SELF-CONCEPT HAS BEEN DEVELOPING UP TO NOW

You may be thinking, "Family? How is my family a part of my academic self-concept?" What about the student who is living away from home for the first time? He or she may think, "My family's not even here. How could they possibly influence what I am doing? Anyhow, one reason I came to college in the first place is that I wanted to have a new experience and live away from my family. Isn't that the point?"

Many students do believe that one of the benefits of college is escape from familial overseers, and surely those students experienced a great sense of freedom during the first week or two that they were away from home. Indeed, some students think of college as a "getaway" vehicle from their families. Regardless, whether we like it or not, our family's influence drives us wherever we go.

Of course, not all students live on campus, away from their families. Students who commute may still live with their families. And adult learners coming back to school face the challenges of being parents of their own families while taking classes. Regardless of the situation, none of us can escape the profound influence of our families.

Whether you live on or off campus, with a family of your own or all alone, your family can affect your academic self-concept. Erin, a college junior, for example, recalls part of her academic autobiography when her familial situation during high school affected her motivation:

> "My brother John was born when I was in the eighth grade. My stepsister Rochelle moved back in when I was in the tenth grade. My mother believes that I reached a new level of laziness in the tenth grade, which she thinks may be partially because she couldn't focus all her attention on making sure I did my homework every night."

Now consider Tricia, who wanted to go away for school because, as she puts it, "Sometimes my mother drives me crazy." Tricia thought about taking a semester off after high school and starting college in January. When she approached her parents with this brilliant idea, her father emphatically said, "Yeah, okay. Not!" Tricia felt her parents placed too many unreasonable expectations on her. She was a straight A student in high school. For her parents, the next natural step was for her to attend college immediately after high school. She felt so burdened by their expectations that during her senior year of high school, she spoke to a counselor to see if she could delay attending college right away. The counselor told her that instead of figuring out what would make *her* happy, she was attempting to please her parents and satisfy *their* expectations of her. Tricia knew for certain that she did not wish to attend college right away, but she did know college *would* be the thing for her at some point in her life. Although she really didn't want to go to school in September, her parents forced her, as she says, to "change her mind."

Now Tricia is embroiled in her first semester. Her past experience surrounding the decision-making process to go to college naturally influences her thoughts and feelings about college now. Essentially, the doubt and confusion concerning whether to attend college is affecting her academic self-concept. Though Tricia did decide to attend college, she is a reluctant participant in the experience. By her own admission, the final decision to go to school ultimately was made to please her parents. If Tricia's heart is not in the endeavor of pursuing a college education, how might this "forced choice" affect the way she approaches her first-year experience? At this point, what recourse does she have?

Student Portrait

Tricia: (laughs) "My mother was like, 'If you don't go to school, you're gonna go to work. You're gonna get out and get a job.' She said that, but it was like, if it came down to it, and I said, 'I'm just gonna do what you said, 'I'm gonna work full-time,' that wouldn't have applied. Do you know what I mean? She said it, but, when it came down to it, was like, 'No, you're going to school.'"

For some families, college is just a natural progression in the educational process; it's what you are supposed to do after high school.

For Tricia's parents, it seems that a college education is compulsory, that is, it is required. For most of us, our educational experience from kindergarten through twelfth grade was compulsory. When it comes time for college, we have a choice, don't we? Apparently, for some families, college is just a natural progression in the educational process; it's what you are supposed to do after high school.

At the opposite end of the spectrum, viewing college as a natural step after high school may not necessarily be the stance all families take. Some students might begin their careers immediately following high school and work for several years before they decide that attending college is an option for them. They may start college for the first time in their mid to late twenties, for example. For other students, they might be the first members of their families to attend college. For them, there can be either an absence of that expectation to attend college or a heightened expectation that they will attend college. Their families might feel that going to college isn't necessarily the best decision, even though these potential college students really wish to attend. Perhaps working after high school would make more sense, for instance. In these families, the children who decide to attend college may be considered rebels or pioneers; they are first-generation college students.

Richard Rodriguez (1998), a well-known first-generation college student, in an essay entitled "The Achievement of Desire," writes extensively about his family's influence on his educational experience and how that influence affected his academic self-concept. Even though you may not be the first person in your family to attend college, Rodriguez' experience shows that your education will likely change your family relationships:

> Quiet at home, I sat with my papers for hours each night. I never forgot that schooling had irretrievably changed my family's life. That knowledge, however, did not weaken ambition. Instead, it strengthened resolve. Those times, I remembered the loss of my past with regret, I quickly reminded myself of all the things my teachers could give me. (They could make me an educated man.) I tightened my grip on pencils and books. I evaded nostalgia. Tried hard to forget. But one does not forget by trying to forget. One only remembers too well that education had changed my family's life. (p. 208)

You may be wondering why Rodriguez had such strong feelings about his education changing his family's life (If so, great. You are displaying intellectual curiosity!). To understand fully his point of view, you'll need to look closely at his background, or "where he's been," just as you'll have to examine your own background. In "The Achievement of Desire," Rodriguez (1998) examines one particular factor that influenced the type of student he was: his Mexican-American heritage. A bilingual student, he describes how, in the second grade, he would come home from school and correct his parents' grammatical mistakes. He recounts an incident in which he proudly announced to his family that his teacher recognized that he was losing all traces of a Spanish accent. For him, this was a sign of academic achievement and success. He discusses these experiences as a way to determine how far his schooling had moved him away from his past. He emphasizes that as a student it was difficult to move between two environments, home and the classroom, because they were at cultural extremes. Do you think his family felt the same way about him losing his accent as he did? Do you think they saw the loss of his accent as an achievement?

For yet other families, the expectation is not only that children attend college, but also that they achieve success beyond what their parents achieved. Take Kay, for example, who feels this pressure as she begins her college experience:

> *"My mother's a lawyer, and I don't want to be a lawyer, so she hasn't influenced me in that way. My father's an accountant, and I hate math. I don't know what I want to be . . . successful. Both my parents are successful. That's what I get from that, and like each generation has to surpass the other generation. I have friends from other Third World countries who have the same problem as to where their parents have reached the peak. We can't . . . so we just have to produce at the same level."*

Here we see Kay grappling with the definition of success and achievement in her family. She is struggling with an aspect of the American dream, the idea that each generation must surpass the previous generation. Her definition of what it means to be successful will certainly affect her behavior in, and attitude about, college, impacting her academic self-concept.

Have you ever stopped to consider the culture of your family of origin and how that may influence your academic self-concept? How does your family define success and achievement, and how might that, in turn, influence your academic self-concept? Students like Erin, Tricia, and Kay often struggle with these questions and don't realize that the answers are closely connected to how their academic self-concepts are formed. Rodriguez recognizes the connection, accepting the premise that education will produce change and transformation. What exactly does change and transformation mean for you?

> **Make It Personal**
>
> What exactly does change and transformation mean for you?

Education is transformative, meaning that education and, more specifically, college will change your life. On one level, the meaning of this statement is rather obvious; you should certainly expect that the courses you'll be taking in the years to come will change the way you think and alter your academic self-concept. You should anticipate that the things that you are learning out of the classroom will have at least as much of an effect on you as what you learn in the classroom. You'll learn much about yourself and others—and you probably wouldn't be surprised to hear that many graduating seniors think they are very different people from those who first walked onto campus four years (give or take) before graduation. While you are at college, try to resist any urge you feel to remain situated in the familiar, in what is most comfortable for you. Allow your education to be transformative. Allow yourself to experience different perspectives and learn from those individuals who are, well, not like you.

RELATING TO YOUR NEW PEERS

ersonality psychologists explain that little can be understood about a person's self-concept without understanding it in relationship to a group of peers to which the person belongs. You have met those who are different from you all over your college campus. These individuals are now your peers. You are taking classes, attending sporting events, and participating in clubs and organizations with your peers. If you are a residential student, you are likely living with your peers.

The way in which you relate to your new peers will affect your academic self-concept and whether you will achieve academic success. Consider Kirsten, who, during her first two years of college, was an average student. She regularly told herself, "I would rather do average and have fun than be a 4.0 student and have no life." She explains how this has been her operating philosophy for as long as she can remember. She found herself believing this theory until the end of the fall semester of her junior year in college. At that point, a new person moved into her suite who had never lived with her before. She played soccer, went out a lot, and had fun, but—surprisingly to Kirsten—she excelled in school as well. Kirsten's new roommate achieved a 3.75 grade point average and made Kirsten realize that her motto may not hold true after all. Kirsten explains, "I believe that I thought it was all right to be average because my friends' grades were also average or below average. I would tell my parents that I was doing fine because I was doing better than or the same as so-and-so."

The new peer in Kirsten's life challenged her belief system and academic self-concept, motivating her to do better. The point here is that you should tune in to the ways in which your peers are influencing your attitudes about yourself and your schoolwork. In this case, the influence had a positive impact on academic self-concept. In the next example, the effect is not so positive.

Ted commuted to campus with a friend of his, Hamid. Neither Hamid nor Ted was very focused on being successful at college. Ted often talked Hamid out of attending class, convincing him to participate in one of many alternate activities. Eating, working out, and criticizing studious peers were all more fun than actually going to class. Both spent the better part of their first semester in college skipping classes and being ignorant of the relationship between their actions and their academic self-concept. Hamid eventually dropped out of college as a result of his poor grades.

As you are establishing friendships in this new environment, ask yourself whether these relationships are contributing to your growth as a student. In the case of Kirsten and Hamid, a single relationship had an enormous impact on their academic self-concept. For other students, a single relationship could have less of an impact. The overall impact of relationships with your friends—whether that means one close friend or 30 teammates—should be contributing to growth. You'll want to consider this as well when you are establishing and maintaining more intimate relationships.

Jono met a girl named Lindsey who changed his attitude toward many things in school. As he remembers, "She calmed me down and I realized that I started to truly fall in love for the first time." Lindsey strongly influenced many of Jono's decisions. "Lindsey helped me take my academics more seriously again because she was much more diligent and had a better work ethic." It is not unusual when you enter into an intimate relationship to adopt some of the behaviors and attitudes of your significant other. In Jono's case, he was fortunate that Lindsey was such a positive influence. Tim, on the other hand, had quite a different experience.

A junior transfer student, Tim reflects upon his less-than-successful sophomore year. What it comes down to, he believes, is a strained relationship with his longtime girlfriend. His transferring to a new school meant moving away from this person whom he'd known for more than four years. The long-distance relationship proved difficult. Conversations on the phone were frequent, but unsatisfying and very expensive. They would see each other on weekends, when Tim made the long journey back home, but these visits meant, inevitably, that the two would have to part yet again. Their experiences and interests were diverging, and they began to acknowledge this reality more with each passing week.

This scenario impacted Tim's ability—or, more accurately, his desire or motivation—to succeed academically. He often found himself thinking about his girlfriend, which kept him from concentrating on papers, exams, reading, and lectures. He wondered whether he'd made the right decision to transfer. Tim and his girlfriend finally decided that it would be in their best interest to stop seeing each other and focus more on their schoolwork.

Intimate relationships can have a profound effect on how people behave. For example, when people are in love, they don't always make logical decisions. Although it is ideal to suggest that our feelings are under our control, clearly with Tim this wasn't always the case. It took him a while to become aware that making the trek home each weekend was taking time away from his schoolwork. Initially, he was unable to see how the relationship was having negative effects on his new college experience. Though Tim really wanted to put his girlfriend out of his mind, he often wasn't able to do so. Instead, he would obsess over her and his decision to transfer, making him unable to focus on school.

It may be easy to dismiss the idea that you would ever allow an intimate relationship to interfere with your academic goals, but it is more realistic to consider that this *is* a possibility. Students who have a critical awareness of how different types of relationships can affect their academic self-concept are more likely to have positive experiences in college. Sarah is one of those students.

Sarah explains how one of the closest, most meaningful relationships she has is with her college roommate, Twee:

> *"About a year ago, I moved into a new suite on campus, and Twee was a transfer student who moved into the room at the same time. Twee is originally from Vietnam and has been in the United States only about four years. When I first met her, I thought she was very nice but didn't think we had enough in common to become close friends. I have realized that you never know who you will become friends with until you give a person a chance. My first impressions are not very trustworthy, and once I got to know Twee, I realized what an awesome person she is. We are now great friends, and I have learned a lot from her. I am so glad she is my roommate and friend."*

Sarah has a great deal of insight into her relationship with Twee. Her detailed account of her friendship provides an apt illustration of how such relationships

Students who have a critical awareness of how different types of relationships can affect their academic self-concepts are more likely to have positive experiences in college.

can profoundly contribute to and organize our experiences, key components of academic self-concept:

> *"I have received a lot from my friendship with Twee. For one thing, she has given me hope in people in general. I yearn to be around honest, friendly, and insightful people, and she is definitely one of them. Meeting her has helped me realize that there are a lot of uplifting people out there; you just have to find them. As a roommate she has been so considerate. She is always around to lend a helping hand and will stop what she is doing to help me if I am in need. She is an optimistic person, and having her around helps keep me optimistic also. I had a rough time during my sophomore year because I was living with people who tended to be very negative and unmotivated. Being around Twee is great for me; motivated and optimistic people help uplift others."*

Sarah goes on to explain the two-sided nature of her relationship with Twee, saying how she hopes Twee views her as a great friend also. She states that when she first met Twee, everything about living on campus, and a lot of things about American culture, were brand new to Twee. She says, "I have been sort of a liaison for her, because I have helped her adjust and adapt to this new experience. I teach her a lot about American culture and have helped her better understand why and how elements of it work." Sarah introduced Twee to people whom she knew and tried to make her feel comfortable at school. Sarah explains how she hopes that she has been a helpful, caring, considerate, and genuine friend to Twee. In Sarah's words, "I hope that she learns a lot from me, for I have learned a lot from her."

Clearly, Sarah has developed a critical awareness of the impact her friendship has had on her overall academic experience. Sarah's ability to self-reflect allows her to see how a close, personal relationship could contribute to her academic self-concept. Her experience with Twee also demonstrates how fulfilling a positive, healthy friendship can be, an example of reciprocal determinism, as explained in Chapter One, in action.

RELATING TO YOUR NEW ENVIRONMENT

Just as you have been asked to give some thought to how your family has affected your developing academic self-concept and how your peers influence you as a student, it will be helpful for you to give some thought to how your relationship with your college or university will evolve, thus influencing your academic self-concept. You probably have not considered the idea that you are beginning a "relationship" with your college or university, but, just like establishing a new friendship as Sarah and Twee did, you will have to put time and effort into getting to know your new environment. The amount of time and effort you choose to put into the relationship with your institution will contribute to the overall quality of that relationship. Again, as with a new friendship, you will have to determine to what level you wish to bring the relationship. Will you put forth minimal effort, thus having a superficial relationship, or will you make and take the time to get to know your institution intimately and reap the benefits of a close, personal relationship? Recall how Sarah was not initially invested in her relationship with Twee, assuming that they did not have enough in common to be close friends, but how later she opened herself up to the experience.

Remember, as Sarah explained, the beginning of a relationship is not always easy. There is sometimes uncertainty when you are establishing a new relationship, but if you decide to work through this, a new relationship can be extremely rewarding.

"Making friends" with campus resources can help you become more comfortable within your new environment.

In this new college or university environment you are facing lots of unknowns. You do not have to face these uncertainties alone. "Making friends" with **campus resources**—departments, people, and programs that support students outside of the classroom—can help you become more comfortable within your new environment. Taking charge of confronting uncertainties and the feelings that go along with them by utilizing campus resources will have positive effects on your academic self-concept and will likely strengthen your relationship with your college or university.

Just how different is this new environment? Well, for one thing, it has a language all its own. When you first arrived to campus, you may have felt like you were on another planet hearing unfamiliar terminology such as "gpa," "prerequisite," "bursar," "provost," and "syllabus." Fortunately, in most colleges and universities, there are people on campus, such as an administrator or a faculty advisor, who can help you interpret this new language. Seek out their advice. A more seasoned student also could prove helpful as you are becoming part of this new academic community.

Remember how Chapter One discussed the expectation that you would take an active role in establishing relationships with faculty members (those people with whom you will primarily interact in the classroom)? Expectations will be placed on you in the larger context of the college or university as well. The central assumption made by staff and administration at many institutions is that you will establish a relationship with your institution outside of the classroom.

Establishing such a relationship means getting involved, taking initiative, and getting more out of your degree than what you learn through taking courses. What these actions entail is that you become an active member of the campus community, by "making friends" with all the resources that will enable you to develop a positive academic self-concept.

Establishing a relationship with your institution requires that you learn more about the environment you are in and consider your position within it. Practically, this means becoming more familiar with the college or university staff and student body by participating in college life, for instance.

Participation in college life can certainly contribute to a more positive academic self-concept. According to Richard Light (2001), a professor at Harvard who has done extensive work on assessment and student success,

> Those students who make connections between what goes on inside and outside the classroom report a more satisfying college experience. The students who find some way to connect their interest in music, for example, either with coursework or with an extracurricular, volunteer activity or both report a qualitatively different overall experience. (p. 14)

Taking part in an organization such as the Make-a-Wish Foundation, for example, will likely affect your academic self-concept. You may develop a keener appreciation of accounting after seeing how important it is to keep track of funds in a philanthropic organization. You may decide to take a management course based on your experience working with other volunteers or a course in elementary education based your experiences with the children you helped. Or, you may conclude that you need to develop a better system for organizing your time and resources and, thus, decide to attend a time management workshop offered by your campus's learning center.

Making connections with what goes on inside and outside of the classroom necessitates getting involved with a variety of activities, which will be found both on and off campus. Making connections and getting involved require a keen sense of how much time you can afford to spend on each activity and still excel in your course work. For instance, a commuter who has a 20-hour-per-week, off-campus internship might learn that she isn't as organized as she thought she was. You will soon find out that fitting it all in is possible with careful, deliberate planning.

Your involvement with clubs and organizations on campus will affect your academic self-concept. Your participation in the many programs available on campus will have similar effects. As with the time management workshop, it would certainly be worth your time to establish relationships with the services that are available on your campus by familiarizing yourself with the locations of, and services provided by, the numerous departments on campus. The counseling office, career services center, registration office, health services department, residence life office, advising office, and public safety department are among the many departments that you are likely to have contact with while on campus. It may surprise you, for example, to discover that the career services center has programming for first-year students to help them explore career opportunities. You may also wish to learn more about student senate and the many other student clubs and organizations. What if Tim had utilized services provided by his college counseling office while he was going through that difficult time with the long-distance relationship? Using those services would have assisted him in handling the stress he was feeling.

How do you find out what services are available? Well, the passive learner would wait for a brochure or flyer to appear in the campus mailbox. An active learner would examine the student handbook and campus directory, visit offices to meet members of the staff, read newsletters and brochures, browse department websites, and talk with other students.

One student, Andy, reported how he wished he had known that his housing office or office of residence life could have helped him with a difficult roommate situation. He assumed for his entire first semester that he just had to live with the bad circumstances. His roommate, Sean, was big on parties. Andy didn't mind having fun occasionally, but he felt Sean had gotten out of control.

Things were fine at the beginning because Sean's "partying" was confined to weekends. Eventually, however, Sean started drinking just about every night. Andy felt he couldn't talk to Sean because he was either drunk or hung over most of the time. Sean also discovered marijuana at school. The big joke on their hallway was that Sean would regularly "wake and bake." Before he climbed out of the top bunk in the morning, he would do a few bong hits. At first it seemed funny, but then Sean started missing classes and work. He would ask Andy to fill him in on notes he missed in the classes they took together and to wake him up in the morning. Andy felt he had enough to do to take care of himself and to keep up with his own work. He was getting tired of acting as Sean's caretaker. When Andy confronted Sean about two-thirds of the way through the first semester, they had a huge argument, which ended with them not speaking to one another. Other people they knew on their hall-way took sides. It was an awful situation that Andy had no idea how to resolve.

Unfortunately, difficult roommate situations can be a common occurrence on college campuses. If only Andy had established a relationship with his resident assistant and/or housing or residence life office, he could have had a much less stressful first semester. The housing office in particular plays a key role in helping students confront and resolve conflicts with roommates. By gaining familiarity with such resources early on, you will be able to efficiently get questions answered and issues resolved. The extent to which you utilize the resources available to you will affect your academic self-concept.

You may never have stopped to consider how your family, friends, and the way you enter into relationships will influence your academic achievement and educational choices. It's extremely important for you to think about your decision to come to college and whether it is the right choice for you. To be successful in college, you must clarify for yourself if this is what you really want and then ask yourself whether you are doing what is necessary to achieve that goal. Thinking about how your family influenced you to make your educational choices will help you begin the process of formulating your academic self-concept.

As you develop and maintain relationships with your peers, you will want to consider the ways in which these relationships are affecting you academically. This critical awareness should be accompanied by the appropriate actions. If certain relationships prove damaging—they limit your study time, distract you during class, and so forth—you should talk with the people involved and if that is unproductive consider ending the relationship.

Finally, as we've argued here, the extent to which you familiarize yourself with and utilize campus resources will affect your academic self-concept. There are many programs and services on your campus; find out which are available and how they can benefit you so that you can maximize their utility.

DISCUSSION QUESTIONS

1. What is your family's definition of academic achievement and success? How does your own definition compare with theirs?

2. Rodriguez (1998) says that his education "irretrievably changed my family's life." What does he mean? Do you agree? Do you anticipate that your education will affect your relationships with family and friends? How will these changes affect your academic self-concept?

3. Reflect on the past four or five years. How did you contribute to the shaping of your school and/or community? How, in turn, did your school and/or community shape you?

4. Reflect on the past four or five years. What contributions have you made to your personal relationships? How have these relationships shaped you?

5. Remember Kirsten's motto: "I would rather do average and have fun than be a 4.0 student and have no life"? Kirsten calls this her "operating philosophy." How might this operating philosophy guide her behavior during her first semester at college?

6. According to Sarah, "motivated and optimistic people help uplift others." Look back on relationships you've had over the last few years. How would you describe the people with whom you surround yourself?

7. How have you begun to establish a relationship with your college or university? How can you develop this relationship in a manner that will have positive effects on your academic self-concept?

8. You read about a difficult roommate situation between Andy and Sean that required discussion to resolve the conflict. When you experience conflict in your relationships, what steps do you take to resolve them? How effective is your approach? Can it be improved?

9. Describe your academic self-concept. Based on your description, predict how you think you will do this semester. What grades do you think you will earn for each class? With what types of activities can you see yourself getting involved?

10. Describe a student with an ideal academic self-concept. What characteristics or qualities would he or she possess?

ACTIVITIES

2.1 Richard Light's (2001) findings show that "those students who make connections between what goes on inside and outside the classroom report a more satisfying college experience." Generate a list of courses and activities that would allow for such a connection. Use your college catalog and student handbook as references for this activity.

2.2 Create an academic autobiography tracing your learning experiences from kindergarten through the twelfth grade. Your autobiography can be a lab report, narrative, formal essay, website, video, or any other appropriate form. A research technique often used by personality psychologists (e.g., Pervin & John, 1997) will be helpful in framing your thinking. The acronym for this technique is "LOTS":

L: *Life record data.* This includes information gathered from report cards and teacher comments.

O: *Observer data.* This includes information from family, friends, and teachers relating to how these individuals view you as a student. This is typically gathered through an interview.

T: Test data. This includes information such as SAT scores, ACT scores, and other standardized test scores.

S: Self-report data. This includes information relating to how you see yourself as a student.

2.3 Choose three campus resources to visit this week. Select one that presented the most poignant information, and create a poster that represents what you learned or an advertisement for the campus resource.

2.4 Select at least one activity to get involved in this semester. What does it take to get involved in the activity? How will you be able to connect this activity with your course work?

2.5 Interview someone you just met—a roommate, a classmate, a professor, an advisor, a tutor—to discover her or his initial impressions of you as a student. Is this how you see yourself? How can you account for any differences?

REFERENCES

Light, R. (2001). *Making the most out of college: Students speak their minds.* Cambridge, MA: Harvard University Press.

Maslow, A. H. (1970). *Motivational personality* (2nd ed.). New York: Harper & Row.

Murray, H. (1938). *Explorations in personality.* New York: Oxford University Press (p. 373).

Pervin, L. A., & John, O. P. (1997). *Personality theory and research* (7th ed.). New York: John Wiley & Sons.

Rodriguez, R. (1998). The achievement of desire. In G. Colombo, R. Cullen, & B. Lisle (Eds.), *Re-reading America: Cultural contexts for critical thinking and writing* (pp. 202–216). Boston: Bedford/St. Martin's.

Planning and Prioritizing

TIME MANAGEMENT AND ACADEMIC GOAL SETTING

Many of you have come to college from high school environments where your teachers and administrators planned and prioritized how you would use your time during the course of a six-hour school day and throughout the school year. These people planned how much time you would spend in your classes, and, within those classes, teachers prioritized your learning activities. Many first-year students get excited at the prospect of going from six hours per day in the highly structured learning environment of high school to a more free and flexible schedule in college. After all, in college, students are expected to be in the classroom an average of only three hours per day.

The change in the structure of the learning environment creates an illusion of free time for first-year students. They think, "Wow, this is great! I'm going to be in school only three hours a day. I'll have tons of time to have fun and maybe even get my work done." Students with this mind-set fail to recognize that time is a limited resource. Like other limited resources, you simply cannot afford to waste it. There are only 24 hours in a day, 7 days in a week, and about 15 weeks in a college semester. You have heard the expression, "time flies," and so too will your first semester at college. You will be surprised at how much you will be expected to accomplish within this limited time frame. Consequently, in college, you will have to do both short-range ("How will I use my time today?") and long-range ("How will I map out my semester?") planning, prioritizing, and goal setting. In other words, you will have to look to the future and plan ahead. The good news is that predicting how you are going to use your time effectively is a skill that can be taught, a skill called **time management.**

IN THIS CHAPTER

- What demands will the various aspects of college life place on your time?

- How will your ability to manage your time affect your academic success?

- What are your academic goals?

- What concrete steps can you take to manage your time most efficiently?

- What would it mean for you to be successful in college? Do you possess the motivation necessary to achieve this success?

- Are you a procrastinator? If so, what type of procrastinator are you?

TIME MANAGEMENT AND COLLEGE SUCCESS

P sychologists have studied time management practices extensively and have concluded that effective time management practices may have a significant influence on college achievement. Consider that intellectual and educational achievement takes time. College students have to complete a large number of tasks in a short period of time. Given this situation, college students tend to feel overloaded and stressed, leading them to consider how they might manage their time more effectively. Researchers report that close to 70 percent of college students desire to manage their time more effectively (Britton & Tesser, 1991).

Britton and Tesser (1991) studied the effect of time management practices on college grades. They observed,

People with modest abilities can accrue substantial lifetime achievements if they focus their abilities effectively on achievable goals in a limited domain over a lengthy period of time. In contrast, some persons of high ability who do not select, prioritize and monitor their goals, sub-goals and tasks, and who therefore seem disorganized accomplish relatively little. (p. 406)

College grades depend on managing the completion of a variety of tasks with varying deadlines. Students are expected to multitask and satisfy the demands of four or five different professors, and grades are, in large part, a factor of their ability to do so.

Britton and Tesser (1991) found that well-developed time management practices positively influence college grades. In fact, in their study, the effects of time management were independent of SAT scores, and even stronger than the influence of SAT scores on grade point average during the first year of college. What does this mean to you? Well, think of your SAT scores and high school grades as a reflection of your abilities. You need to channel the abilities that got you into college productively; otherwise, those abilities will bring you only so far. The key is to "focus those abilities effectively on achievable goals" (Britton & Tesser, 1991, p. 406). That's where sound time management practices come in, and the good news is, such practices can be learned.

SELF-REGULATING YOUR OWN LEARNING

T he question is, then, "What are sound time management practices, and how and when do I implement them?" Naturally, in college, much of your free time will be spent reading and studying. That is not to say you won't have time to relax and have some fun, but you must balance study and leisure time. This is difficult because of the illusion of free time previously mentioned. Because you will be in the classroom an average of just three hours per day, you will have to decide how to use the rest of your time. You will have to **self-regulate** your own learning. Unlike in high school where you may have had teachers and parents helping to manage your reading and studying time, in college this process is *your* responsibility.

You may be surprised to learn that when professors structure their courses, they do so with the expectation that students will spend an average of 2 to 3 hours studying outside of class for every hour spent in the classroom. If you have five classes, then, at approximately 3 hours per week, the expectation is that you'll be doing out-of-class work for 30 to 45 hours per week. You can see why many people consider college a full-time job (where the currency earned is knowledge and sense).

Many students, such as Kirsten in Chapter Two, when they consider the demands on their time, immediately consider such demands unreasonable: "There just aren't enough hours in the day. How can I spend that much time on schoolwork and still have a life?" Rest assured, if you manage your time effectively, you can have both a fulfilling college life and a handle on your schoolwork.

Consider the 8–8–8 Formula

There are 24 hours in a day. Let's say the average human adult needs 8 hours of sleep per night, give or take. You would like 8 hours of leisure time, time you can spend by yourself or with others. Go ahead. Take it. You still have 8 hours remaining. If you spend 3 hours in classes, you have 5 hours left for doing out-of-class work, in other words, 8 hours of schoolwork. That is the **8–8–8 formula**.

Now, take those 5 hours per day for out-of-class work and multiply that by 5, for you'll be doing this for each of the days in the week. That equals 25 hours of schoolwork. On the weekends, you'll have to find another 5–20 hours for studying, so you can reach that 30- to 45-hour-per-week expectation. Think of 30 hours as the minimum and 45 hours as a maximum.

If this seems rather formulaic, it is. The purpose of the 8–8–8 formula is to show you that there *is* enough time in the day if you are prepared to manage your time. There will be times when you will need to do more studying and forego some of your leisure time. Your time commitments will change depending on the demands of your classes and the time of the semester. During midterms and finals, for example, you may be working 45 hours per week outside of class. You may wish to "stockpile" your homework hours during the week and take weekends off from studying. You may wish to reserve your leisure hours for the weekends. The possibilities of how you will plan and organize your time are endless. You will have to tailor your time management practices to your personality, lifestyle choices, and college activities. It's all up to you, and a positive attitude counts! It is likely, in fact, that you'll begin to blur the lines between leisure time and study time. You could, for example, develop a penchant for reading when you have been exposed to new disciplines, ideas, and cultures.

You will have to tailor your time management practices to your personality, lifestyle choices, and college activities.

You may observe that the 8–8–8 formula is rather straightforward and, on the surface, doesn't necessarily account for unique situations in which students may find themselves. What if students have to work 10 hours per week or if they are participating in team sports, for example? Where would they find the time in the 8–8–8 formula for such activities that are not clearly outlined by the formula? Well, these students would be faced with having to make some difficult decisions. Let's say a varsity tennis player has team practice from 3:00 to 6:00 P.M. every day or another student has a job on campus that takes up 3 hours daily. From where within the 8–8–8 formula would they "borrow" these hours?

Well, most experts on sleep would likely agree that taking time from healthy sleep habits and operating in sleep deprivation mode would not be the best solution. Sleep deprivation results in lower tolerance toward fighting off infection, for instance. With the pace of a college semester, you can't afford to get sick. How about borrowing from those 8 hours dedicated to classes and schoolwork? That may work during some weeks but overall likely is not the best solution. Unfortunately, what none of us like to do is dip into our leisure time, but participating in a demanding activity such as a varsity sport or having to work out of financial need may necessitate that difficult choice.

Remember, though, that there is a payoff for this dedication and hard work. A typical college semester is 15 weeks, so forfeiting some leisure time for that distinct period of time may be well worth the sacrifice—at the end of all of those 15-week semesters, you will likely have a degree in hand.

HOW TO MANAGE YOUR TIME

Now that you are aware of the importance of managing your time while at college, it is time to look at some practical methods of doing so. These methods are discussed as they relate to the *three major roadblocks to successful studying,* identified by Alan Lakein (1973), a Harvard MBA graduate who coined the term "time management": (1) the lack of planning and organization, (2) the lack of a proper place to study, and (3) procrastination.

Be Sure to Plan and Organize

To get some control of your life in college, you need to plan for both long- and short-term commitments. Essentially, planning for these commitments means setting academic goals that you intend to meet. The best way to do this is to make schedules in which you carefully record your goals, try out the schedules, and revise them as necessary. Your plan may not work perfectly at first, but you can improve it as you learn how much studying you need to do and gain insight into your own ability to organize and meet the goals you set for yourself. What follows is a **three-tier time management system** for college students; the three tiers are the semester schedule, the weekly schedule, and the daily schedule.

Create a semester schedule

A **semester schedule** will help you look at the entire semester. Use a daily planner, an electronic planner, or other form of calendar that shows you the 15-or-so week time span of the semester. Using this calendar, record due dates for papers, projects, and presentations, and enter midterm and final exam information next to the appropriate dates and times.

Doing so will help you think about the total amount of work you are required to do to be successful in your courses. To complete a semester schedule, you will need to look closely at your course outlines and syllabi. This is a beneficial exercise for two reasons. First, you will be more aware of the work expected in each particular course. Second, and equally, or even more, important, however, is that you will see where work overlaps across courses. For example, you will undoubtedly have weeks when you will have a paper due in more than one class as well as an exam. Because much of this information is available to you from the start, you can plan weeks in advance, have a less stressful time getting things done, and do a better job in the process.

Now that you've entered this important information in your calendar, you are ready to consider how much time it will take you to prepare for each of these papers, projects, presentations, and exams. After all, you don't expect to start working on a project or studying for an exam the day before your work will be collected, do you? Such last-minute work is typically of poor quality and results in an anxious student dissatisfied with the experience. Cramming for an exam usually results in a subpar performance; the more serious effect, however, is that cramming results in short-term retention of just some of the information. Assuming that you are at college to learn and retain information, such study techniques should be avoided. To avoid putting yourself in this situation, estimate the amount of time you will need to spend on particular assignments. Establish deadlines for finishing each one, and enter the dates on your calendar. The key is to be as specific as possible and generous with your time allotments.

Let's use a biology midterm as an example. How might you work backward from the date of this exam so that you aren't waiting until the last minute to cram? Let's say there are four weeks of material to be digested before the exam. You could try studying for the exam during this entire four-week period. Doing so might involve placing notes in your daily planner such as "Review biology notes" for days between classes. You might also include notes such as "Take chapter self-test" each Friday. Continual review and self-testing will allow you to get your questions answered—whether through consulting the textbook or asking your professor during class or office hours. Chapter Six outlines this technique in more detail, and Chapter Five includes information regarding how to break up written assignments into more manageable units.

When you break up large projects into smaller units, enter minideadlines in your semester calendar.

Many institutions now offer a free calendar function to students via the campus intranet. This function allows you to input your semester schedule on-line with easy access to the events going on around campus. Consider taking advantage of such a resource if it is available.

Exhibit 3.1 shows part of a semester schedule created by Kendra, a first-year student. Has Kendra used the advice offered thus far? How could her semester schedule be improved?

EXHIBIT 3.1	*Sample partial semester schedule.*	
MONDAY	**TUESDAY**	**WEDNESDAY**
1 Felicity's 18th! Meetings: Dr. Hasseler—3 p.m. Father Joe—3:30 p.m. Poetry reading—7 p.m. S.A.I.L.—7 p.m.—Papitto	**2** Proposal due—Psych. Business exam! Finance Assoc.—4:30 p.m. ΔΣΠ—7 p.m.—Papitto	**3** Room inspection—6 p.m. Article summaries— Microeconomics Tutor training—ACE—3 p.m.
8 Columbus Day—No classes! Research for Psych. 1) find sources 2) begin notes (25 cards)	**9** No Liberal Arts Seminar Ch. 7—Psych. Business meets in library Finance Assoc.—4:30 p.m.	**10** Ch. 21—Microeconomics Tutor training—ACE—3 p.m. Confirmation class—4:45 p.m.
15 Take-home exam issued in Microeconomics—Due Friday Psych. research (25 cards) ΔΣΠ—Elections S.A.I.L.—7 p.m.—Papitto	**16** Ch. 9—Psych. Ch. 14—Business Overview & planning document due—Business Finance Assoc.—4:30 p.m.	**17** Economics exam due 10-19 Tutor training—ACE—3 p.m. Confirmation class—4:45 p.m.
22 Psych. research—complete ΔΣΠ S.A.I.L.—7 p.m.—Papitto	**23** Ch. 11—Psych. BNA #3 Due } Business B.P. Day } Finance Assoc.—4:30 p.m.	**24** Ch. 24—Microeconomics Dinner w/Marcus @ 6:30 p.m. Tutor training—ACE—3 p.m. Confirmation class—4:45 p.m.

Create a weekly schedule

Many students are shocked into good study habits when they see how much good study time they aren't using. If you feel you must find more study time, try making a **weekly schedule** to see how much of your time is available for study.

Write in fixed commitments such as classes, labs, and job hours. Then list times for life support which includes eating, sleeping, grooming, transportation, and outside employment. Next, tentatively block out large spaces of time for studying. Within those times, schedule your highest-priority subjects when you usually feel the most alert. This time of day will vary according to the individual; some people are more alert at night, whereas others do their best work early in the day. Finally, be sure to plan time for fun and relaxation. You cannot work every minute, so be fair to yourself by scheduling definite times for recreation. Don't feel guilty about using this time for fun! Soon you will see that scheduling time for fun and relaxation is a vital component to following through on your schedule.

Exhibit 3.2 shows Kendra's weekly schedule. As you can see, the grid she has used is easy to duplicate; consider using this or a similar format to construct your own weekly schedule.

Create a daily schedule, or "to-do lists"

Planning for an entire semester and looking at when you'll do course work during a typical week are important activities in time management. Eventually, though, you'll need to do this work, taking it one day at a time. A **daily schedule** or a "**to-do**" **list** will help you achieve the goals set down in the semester and weekly schedules. You can make weekly and daily to-do lists on a separate sheet of paper, or log them in an electronic organizer that contains date book and to-do list functions.

Remember to refer to your semester and weekly schedules to prioritize your lists. You'll probably want to carry your to-do list with you so that you don't lose track of what you need to accomplish each day. After all, you'll be answering to yourself regarding this list. It is up to you to meet the deadlines you've set for yourself. Focus on completing your priorities first, crossing off tasks as soon as you finish them. Exhibit 3.3 shows an example of a to-do list. Has the student prioritized her time? How might this list help or hinder her time management?

Typing or writing things out in this manner not only forces you to plan your time, but also, in effect, causes you to make a promise to yourself to *do* what you have written down. Adherence to the schedules and lists you've created is critical; here, again, your attitude is important. You must have the drive to implement your plan and the perseverance to follow it daily. Don't let an impromptu party in your residence hall extinguish your plan to read microeconomics and *Black Picket Fences* Thursday night.

EXHIBIT 3.2	*Sample weekly schedule.*

SCHEDULE FOR THE WEEK OF: *October 1 to October 5*

	MONDAY	TUESDAY	WEDNESDAY	THURSDAY	FRIDAY
8:00		Psychology 8:00–9:15		Psychology 8:00–9:15	
:15					
:30					
:45	Breakfast 8:30–9:00		Breakfast 8:30–9:00		Breakfast 8:30–9:00
9:00	Math Reasoning 9:00–9:50		Math Reasoning 9:00–9:50		Math Reasoning 9:00–9:50
:15		Breakfast 9:15–10:00		College Relations Office 9:30–11:00	
:30					
:45	Homework 9:50–11:30				Homework 9:50–11:30
10:00		Homework 10:00–11:00	College Relations Office 10:00–12:00		
:15					
:30					
:45					
11:00		Hon. Intro. to Business 11:00–12:15		Hon. Intro. to Business 11:00–12:15	
:15					
:30	Lunch 11:30–12:00				Lunch 11:30–12:50
:45					
12:00	Microeconomics 12:00–12:50		Microeconomics 12:00–1:15		
:15					
:30		Hon. Liberal Arts Seminar 12:30–1:45		Hon. Liberal Arts Seminar 12:30–1:45	
:45					
1:00	College Relations Office 1:00–2:30				College Relations Office 1:00–4:00
:15			Homework 1:15–6:00		
:30					
:45		Homework 1:45–4:30		Lunch 1:45–2:15	
2:00					
:15				Homework 2:15–6:30	
:30					
:45					
3:00	Homework 3:00–6:00				
:15					
:30					
:45					
4:00					Homework 4:00–6:00
:15					
:30		Finance Association 4:30–6:00			
:45					
5:00					
:15					
:30					
:45					
6:00	Dinner 6:00–7:00	Dinner 6:00–6:30	Dinner 6:00–6:30		Dinner 6:00–6:30
:15					
:30					
:45		Homework 6:30–10:00	Homework 6:30–10:00	Personal Productivity Software 6:30–8:30	Homework 6:30–10:00
7:00	SAIL— Students Advancing in Leadership 7:00–9:00				
:15					
:30					
:45					
8:00					
:15					
:30					
:45				Dinner 8:30–9:00	
9:00	Homework 9:00–10:00			Homework 9:00–10:00	
:15					
:30					
:45					
10:00					

EXHIBIT 3.3   *Sample to-do list.*

THINGS TO DO

Week of: 10-3 to 10-7

Monday

Math Reasoning 1—Math project—Due Wed.

Microeconomics—Article summaries

Meetings—Prof. Hasseler—3 p.m.

Father Joe—3:30 p.m.

Ch. 19—pp. 455–460, notes

Other Stuff—Intro to Business Test tomorrow

Psych. paper proposal for tomorrow

Poetry Reading—7 p.m.—MRC4

Tuesday

Psychology—Test Thursday

Intro. to Business—Test today

Liberal Arts Seminar—No class today!—

   Read pp. 1–75 Black Picket Fences (Thurs.)

Other Stuff—Microeconomics: Finish notes, Ch. 19

Finish math project

Wednesday

Math Reasoning 1—Hw #9: 1–4

   #2, 9, 17, 40, 47

Read pp. 52–54 Do #1–5—#9, 19

   pp. 55–58 Do #6

Microeconomics—Ch. 20—Notes,

   pp. 482–490, article summaries

Other Stuff—Read pp. 76–152—Black Picket Fences

     Psych. exam tomorrow!

     Business plan brainstorming

Thursday

Psychology—Exam Today!—create outline for paper

Intro. to Business—Ch. 13—pp. 381–395

Liberal Arts Seminar—finish Black Picket Fences

   for next Thursday

Other Stuff—Microeconomics: Finish Ch. 20,

   notes, and article summaries

Friday

Math Reasoning 1—Hw #10: 2-1

   #6, 7, 26, 28, 35, 38, 42, 45

*Friday: Call ACE for appt. next Tuesday

Microeconomics—Project

Other Stuff—Rough draft of midterm

Saturday/Sunday

Plan for a Suitable Place to Study

Along with planning your time, you need to *plan carefully for a suitable place or places to study*. Studying in your residence hall can be problematic; there are too many distractions: friends coming in and out of your room, televisions and radios blaring, and video games, to mention a few. It would be better to study in a quiet place, preferably with a desk and chair, and a place to spread out your books and papers. You need adequate light and a comfortable temperature for optimum productivity.

The most important thing about your study place is that it be used only for study. When you go there, you should automatically be able to use your habitual pattern of studying to help you start work immediately without a long warm-up period. Use this study space for your large blocks of study time. You may need other study places; these could be used for shorter study periods such as time between classes.

There are many places where you can *take advantage of shorter spans of study time*. You can listen to a tape in your car as you drive to class as a way to review lectures or other study material. You can take advantage of an empty classroom as a place to review your notes before your next class. Or, you can study outdoors under a tree in between classes or in a waiting room before an appointment. If you plan ahead by making study cards for review, or if you select a textbook section you need to read, you can accomplish a great deal of routine work while waiting in a number of places.

Even though we have repeatedly stressed the importance of managing your time well so that you may read and study, many students confess that they don't know exactly how to study or, as the weeks of their first semester march by, they realize that the study habits that they used in high school simply aren't working in college. Not to worry, though—learning college-level study strategies is addressed at length in Chapter Four. For now, know that it's important to be sure you have set enough time aside for studying.

Learn to Avoid Procrastination

After you have scheduled your study time and have found a satisfactory place to study, you may still run into the third roadblock: putting off completing tasks, despite the fact that you've designated them as top priority.

In his book *How to Get Control of Your Time and Your Life,* Alan Lakein (1973) states that, even if you set up high-priority activities, you may have difficulty completing them for several reasons. First, you **procrastinate**; that is, you do not start or work on your important project, because it seems too complex, difficult, time-consuming, or overwhelming. Instead, you work on some lower-priority activities because you can see immediate results.

To avoid procrastinating on a research paper, for instance, you can take steps toward starting immediately by spending some time thinking about the assignment and writing down some ideas, talking with your instructor about the topic, or spending a few minutes looking for sources of information in the library. These activities help you get started and break up the task into smaller, more manageable pieces.

After you begin your project, you will still need to keep yourself on track and follow through. Lakein (1973) suggests a number of activities that will help you get back on track:

- getting more information, perhaps by talking with your instructor, or by reading more sources
- setting a next step—this will keep you involved
- taking rest breaks and work breaks
- setting a deadline: committing yourself to a series of actions at definite times
- giving yourself a pep talk
- not letting fear or lack of self-confidence stop you
- learning to stress benefits and reward yourself for a period of good work
- being aware of when you are running away from your priority activity

He also offers a list of some escapes to avoid, including

- indulging yourself with something you like to do instead of working
- socializing
- reading irrelevant material
- doing something that you could delegate to others
- running away, such as going out shopping
- daydreaming

These are great suggestions, but why is it that many of us find it extremely difficult to reach the goals that we've set for ourselves? It's fine to create plans and schedules (e.g., the semester and weekly schedules, and daily to-do lists) and to carefully and deliberately record academic goals, yet it sometimes seems impossible to *attain* the goals. Why is this?

> ### Make It Personal
>
> Why is it that many of us find it extremely difficult to reach the goals that we've set for ourselves?

MOTIVATION AND PROCRASTINATION

nextricably linked to time management and academic goal setting are the concepts of motivation and procrastination. Students may be able to motivate themselves to the point where they've planned how they'll use their time, and they've even clearly set the academic goals that they'd like to achieve, yet many just don't follow through and use their schedules, even though they've made them. They just can't seem to get motivated. Why is this? What *is* motivation exactly?

According to psychologists, motivation is "the need or desire that serves to energize behavior and direct it toward a goal" (Myers, 2002, p. 335). For our purposes, let's think about goals in terms of academic demands: going to classes, taking notes, reading, starting and completing projects, writing papers, and studying for tests and exams. Let's think of motivation in terms of reaching these goals to the best of your ability. Some individuals have the "need to succeed."

Others are less driven. One psychologist, Murray (1938), described the "need to succeed" as **achievement motivation** or the desire for significant accomplishment, for mastering skills or ideas, for control, and for rapidly attaining a high standard.

People who have the need to succeed in college, or other endeavors for that matter, have some traits in common. They enjoy moderately difficult tasks for which success is attainable, yet attributable to their skills and effort. They are persistent, eager, and self-disciplined (Myers, 2002). Ultimately, whether you decide to engage in the pursuit of achievement in college depends, to an extent, on your attitude, the extent to which you are prepared to claim your education, and how you look at and tackle your academic goals. All you need, then, is a positive attitude, right? Not exactly. In addition to having a positive attitude along with the need and/or desire to do the right thing, you need to follow through. Unfortunately, good intentions and a positive attitude don't always translate into the desired behavior.

Procrastinators Believe Their System Works

Many college students claim that they are particularly motivated to get their schoolwork done when they are under pressure. These students say, "I do my best work when I am under pressure, like the night before my paper is due." This is a common credo of the procrastinator. Just as motivation is related to time management, so is procrastination.

Think of motivation as an expression of your attitude toward achievement and procrastination as a behavior.

Think of *motivation* as an expression of your attitude toward achievement and *procrastination* as a behavior. *Procrastination* is putting off doing something until a future time or needlessly postponing or delaying doing something. If you have the attitude that you can't get motivated until you are under pressure, then you certainly will needlessly postpone or delay doing that paper until the night before it is due. In a sense, when students tell themselves they work best under pressure, they are giving themselves permission to procrastinate. In reality, they are deceiving themselves.

Procrastination Has Consequences

There is a deceptive component to procrastination. When you procrastinate, you put yourself in the position of lying to yourself and others. Many professors will tell you that students lie to them when it comes time to take a test or turn in a paper or project. At these times, it seems an inordinate number of relatives are dying, cars are having mechanical problems, and computers are crashing. Is it merely a coincidence that natural deaths, dead car batteries, and computer viruses are on the rise during exam time or around due dates posted on a syllabus? That is highly doubtful. Such excuses indicate, for the most part, that students have procrastinated and need to lie themselves out of the precarious situations they have created.

Identifying a lie that you've told to another person is a lot easier than figuring out when you are lying to yourself. Experts estimate that most people lie at least 25 times in a single day! It may be obvious when you've lied to someone else, but how many of those 25 times are you lying to yourself? One of the keys to combating procrastination is having an awareness of your patterns of lying. Experts identify three broad categories for why people lie:

1. To make others feel better about themselves: "No, that outfit doesn't make you look fat."
2. To boast about ourselves and make ourselves look better: "I didn't even crack that book and still got an A on the exam."
3. To protect ourselves: "I don't feel like studying right now; I'll start after dinner."

The third type of lie has the greatest influence on procrastination behavior. We may not feel motivated to study, so to safeguard against having to think about the work that has piled up, we convince ourselves that it's okay to begin later, such as after dinner. Do you have a sense into what category your lies fall?

Besides lying, procrastination has other serious consequences. It is no surprise that researchers have found that procrastinators start studying significantly later, and thereby study fewer hours, than more motivated nonprocrastinators (Lay & Burns, 1991). The result is obvious. Less time spent studying results in lower grades and less learning. This research finding is contrary to procrastinators' mantra that they work well under pressure; what they are actually saying is that the work gets done despite having been repeatedly put off. That may be true, but *completing* a set of readings or finishing a research paper does not mean that either was done *well*.

Indeed, the tendency to procrastinate negatively impacts grades. One researcher found that procrastination, like time management practices, has a stronger influence on college grades than high school grades and SAT scores combined (Wesley, 1994). College admissions offices use SAT scores and high school grades as predictors of student achievement, yet these two indicators typically account for only about 30 percent of the picture when it comes to first-semester college grades. What this all means is that no matter what kind of academic history you bring to college, procrastinating ultimately will impede your academic performance.

Gaining Control Over Procrastination

If you accept the idea that procrastination has a significant negative impact on grades, you should be interested in what you can do to combat procrastination. The first step is to identify common procrastination behaviors—develop a keen awareness of how *you* procrastinate—including any behaviors that produce problems with time management. The following list of procrastinatory behaviors is not exhaustive, but it will surely help you get started identifying your own. Do any of these look familiar? You may wish to check off those that apply to you.

1. Waiting until the last minute to do things.
2. Waiting until a crisis arises or the semester has ended before taking action.
3. Not setting personal deadlines and sticking to them.
4. Doing things quickly, but incorrectly, thus having to redo them.
5. Spending a lot of time on routine and trivial things.
6. Not establishing a daily schedule.
7. Failing to prioritize tasks; treating everything as if it were equally important.
8. Not saying "no" to requests or invitations.
9. Spending time socializing instead of working.
10. Reading things unessential to the work at hand.
11. Spending too much time on the telephone.
12. Not having clear goals or objectives.
13. Seldom asking other people to help, failing to delegate tasks.
14. Failing to listen to or read instructions.
15. Trying to do the "perfect" project, paper, etc.
16. Overscheduling, taking on too many commitments, overextending.
17. Engaging in paper shuffling.
18. Not anticipating the emergency situation, not realizing a full schedule doesn't accommodate the unexpected.

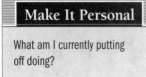

Make It Personal

What am I currently putting off doing?

You may feel like hitting the panic button at this point. Many students admit that they check off every item on the list and feel like lost causes. Not to worry. Every human being procrastinates; it's not easy to **delay gratification**, or restrain our impulses. It's far easier to put fun first. Self-disciplined people find ways to put work first and then have fun. Remember, those with high achievement motivation are self-disciplined.

Now that you've begun to think of the ways in which you have procrastinated in the past, you would do well to think of how you may be procrastinating at the present. Ask yourself these questions:

- What am I currently putting off doing?
- What have I procrastinated about in the past?
- Does a pattern emerge? In other words, are there certain types of tasks that I tend to put off?
- How will I be aware that I am procrastinating?
- Do I engage in **replacement activities**, in other words, activities other than those I should be doing?

Identify your replacement activities

Most replacement activities are quite easy to identify; these usually include the obvious such as watching too much TV, playing video games, using instant messaging, or just hanging out in your room with friends. Students usually have their favorites. Often, however, it is difficult to identify other types of replacement activities, because many times, they are masked by productivity. For example, you may have to do your laundry, clean your room, go to the bank, check your email, or mail your monthly bills. All of these tasks are important and necessary, but are they priorities?

Take Jack, for example. After a rough morning of class, he decides on an early workout. He has a big management exam tomorrow and thinks that working out will help him get his brain energized. An hour and a half later, Jack is headed back to his residence hall, a bit sore, but ready to tackle the five chapters he has put off reading. When he finally gets to his room, though, he sees piles of clothes on his desk and bed. "Can't study in this mess," he thinks, and he begins to get his laundry together for a wash and dry. "This won't take long," he says to himself, "and when I'm done, I'll be able to concentrate on management." The next two hours in the laundry room prove to be a social success. He catches up with some of his hall mates that he hasn't seen in a week and hears about last night's "incident" from reliable sources. Though he realizes that it's getting late, Jack tells himself that he'll get to reading after dinner. When seven o'clock does roll around, Jack begins reading chapter seven—the problem is it takes him an hour and a half to get through its 40 pages. He decides that he'll do more skimming for the next four chapters. This is faster, for sure, but now he's not certain he understands the material. At 2 A.M., Jack is beginning to think he won't do so well on his exam. At least he's got clean laundry.

Students often engage in productive activities, such as doing laundry, to put off doing more important things, such as reading a chapter that is due the following day. They make themselves feel better because an important task was accomplished, and now they can cross "laundry" off of their to-do list. Engaging in these types of activities makes the person feel they've accomplished something, but, in essence, what they've really done is avoided their top priorities. Students who do this are "productive procrastinators." They'll clean their rooms (a noble activity) and one or two hours will go by before they realize they were actually wasting important homework time. This is yet another aspect of the deceptive nature of procrastination, and why it can be so hard to identify. Combating procrastination, then, necessitates establishing some effective behavioral patterns and habits.

Try antiprocrastination behaviors and habits

In college, those who effectively manage their time well have the ability to delay gratification and combat procrastination. They are able to do so by abiding by some basic principles, outlined here, some of which have been mentioned previously:

1. *Study in a regular place at a regular time.* Establishing habits of study is extremely important. Knowing when you are going to study, and where, saves a lot of time in making decisions about studying. Locate a study place that is comfortable for you and has few distractions (e.g., family, friends, noise, phones, TVs, video games, instant messaging, email).

2. *Study during your periods of maximum alertness.* Some people are more efficient in the early mornings and others in the afternoon or early evenings. Find out when you are the most effective, and utilize those periods to do your studying so you can be the most productive, if possible.

3. *Limit your blocks of study time to no more than two hours at a time on any one course.* After one and a half to two hours of studying, you begin to tire rapidly and your ability to concentrate diminishes. Taking a break and then switching to studying for another course will provide the change necessary to maintain your efficiency.

4. *Set specific goals for each study unit.* When you record your goals on a schedule, write specifically what you are planning to accomplish during the study period. For example, don't just write "do math" or "study" or "read." Instead, put "do math problems 1–10."

5. *Plan enough study time to do justice to each subject.* Again, most college professors require about two to three hours of work per week per credit in the course. By multiplying your credit load by three, you can get a good idea of the time you should set aside for studying. Of course, if you are a slow reader, or have other study deficiencies, you may need to plan more time in order to maximize your learning potential.

6. *Attempt to complete all assignments as soon as possible after class.* Check over lecture notes while they are still fresh in your mind. Start assignments while the memory of the assignment is still accurate.

7. *Provide for a spaced review.* This means schedule a regular, weekly time period when you will review the work in each of your courses and be sure you are up to date. This review should be cumulative, covering briefly all the work done thus far in the semester. Studies show that consistent cumulative reviewing over the course of a semester has a far greater impact on memory and retention than the "cramming" method.

8. *Plan a schedule of balanced activities.* As suggested in the 8–8–8 formula, you should be sure to include time for social activities when you construct a weekly study schedule. Seeing that you have some fun things to look forward to will motivate you to study. Build in rewards for yourself for a job well done.

9. *Trade time—don't steal it.* When unexpected events arise that take up time you had planned for study, decide immediately where you can find the time to make up the study missed and adjust your schedule for that week.

These antiprocrastination behaviors should sound like sensible suggestions, but what if you can't get yourself to try them? If this is the case, you are probably a **die-hard procrastinator.** Die-hard procrastinators tend to get stuck in a rut to the point where they are completely immobilized. One way to figure out if you fall into this category of procrastinators is to ask yourself if you typically use your snooze alarm in the morning. Think about it; those who use snooze alarms are procrastinating waking up! Let's face it. If you procrastinate getting out of bed, you meet the criteria. You are a die-hard procrastinator.

David D. Burns, M.D. (1992) knows well the psyches of diehards. He wrote an essay entitled "Stop Putting It Off!: A Five-Step Plan to Get Even the Most Die-Hard Procrastinator Moving Again" for his book, *The Feeling Good Handbook*. In his essay, he explains that many of us find ourselves procrastinating from time to time. He cites a survey conducted by Esther Rothblum and colleagues of 342 students at the University of Vermont; nearly half admitted they procrastinated on writing term papers. The study found that "though the reasons varied, the most frequent explanation was fear of failure" (Burns, 1992, p. 87). How can this possibly make sense? Why would people afraid of failing put off doing their work? Instead, you would think they'd overcompensate and work extra hard in an attempt to be productive.

Think of it this way. Jason perceives writing a term paper as an arduous task. He doesn't know how to begin, so rather than tackle the job, he avoids it. Indeed, there is an avoidance component to procrastination. Every time he thinks about starting the paper, he gets a little anxious, because he is unsure where to start. His anxiety fuels the fear of failure. As a college student, he feels it is his job to know how to write a term paper. He avoids asking for help because he doesn't want to be "found out." What if the professor realizes he has no idea how to do the necessary research to get the required sources for his term paper? This thought just adds to the anxiety. Every time he thinks about the assignment, he becomes more and more nervous and afraid that he won't be able to do well on the paper. He then says to himself, "I'll just deal with this later. I have plenty of time before my term paper is due."

Anxiety, the feeling of being unsettled but unsure why, is difficult to face. Instead of facing our fears head-on, we tend to avoid the source of our anxiety—in this case, the dreaded term paper. Sigmund Freud proposed that we use what he called **defense mechanisms**, a way to distort reality to reduce our anxiety. A defense mechanism that is frequently employed by college students is **rationalization**. Rationalization occurs when we justify our undesirable behaviors with excuses (Myers, 2002). Jason justifies not beginning his term paper because he rationalizes that he has "plenty of time." Essentially, he distorts reality to ward off the anxiety created by not knowing how to get the paper started. As each week passes by, he allows himself less and less time to accomplish the task. He keeps telling himself that time is on his side. He never considers the idea that perhaps the term paper was assigned during the first week of the semester because the professor designed the assignment knowing that a decent term paper would take an entire semester to complete. The reality is Jason *doesn't* have plenty of time to complete his term paper.

Remember Kirsten from Chapter Two, Developing Academic Self-Concept? She was also quite adept at rationalization, demonstrated when she said, "I would rather do average and have fun than be a 4.0 student and have no life." Students use rationalization to give themselves "permission" to behave and act in a certain way. Jason tells himself that time is on his side to permit himself to continue putting off the task of working on his term paper, and Kirsten convinces herself

> ### Make It Personal
>
> Do you use rationalization to justify procrastination?

that 4.0 students don't have fun, so she can continue being average instead of working toward her potential.

If you employ the defense mechanism of rationalization as a means of giving yourself permission to continue your procrastination behaviors, as die-hard procrastinators tend to do, then you'll benefit from this five-step plan, from Burns (1992):

> 1. *Expect difficulties.* Those who procrastinate often assume that successful people achieve their goals without frustration, self-doubt and failure. . . . Highly productive people . . . *assume* they'll encounter obstacles; when they do, they persevere until they overcome them. (p. 88)

Jason, for example, assumed that as a college student he should already know how to do research for a term paper. He saw not knowing how to conduct research as an obstacle he couldn't readily overcome. He never entertained the idea that some of his classmates might feel the same way. Instead of procrastinating, though, it is likely that the successful students in Jason's class persevered and overcame this obstacle. Perhaps they visited the professor during his or her office hours; maybe they went to a reference librarian and asked for assistance or visited their college's writing or tutoring center; they may have even asked upper-class students how they dealt with writing their first term paper.

> 2. *Do a cost-benefit analysis.* When you're ducking an important task, weigh the advantages of procrastinating against the disadvantages. (Burns, p. 88)

Marcia admits to putting off just about everything, including making it to all of her classes. She describes herself as "lazy" and bored with schoolwork. Rather than study, she explains,

> *"Even if I know an exam is approaching within a week or that reading regularly would be a good idea for a class, I refuse to do the work. On nights that I have a paper due or an exam in class the next day, you can usually find me in my bedroom reorganizing my closet, making my bed, or vacuuming my floor. If I have done all of those things recently, I will lie down and watch TV, do the dishes, or clean the bathroom."*

Instead of going to class, sometimes Marcia continues her cleaning binges or wanders around, talking to friends.

Marcia essentially uses the rationalization that she's lazy and bored with schoolwork to avoid studying for a test. Clearly, Marcia is not a lazy person. Cleaning and organizing take a great deal of work and energy. For Marcia, these are her replacement activities, but why can't she direct that same energy toward her schoolwork? Frustrated with her procrastinatory behavior, Marcia decides to do a cost–benefit analysis regarding her behavior. It turns out that Marcia was procrastinating by doing more than just spring cleaning.

Marcia first lists the advantages of her procrastination:

It makes me feel like I've accomplished something when I clean and organize:
Benefit: A neat closet makes it much easier to find an outfit to wear.
Benefit: A clean bathroom makes me feel more at home, less stressed.

Benefit: Watching TV helps me escape the pressures of school.

Benefit: There has to be space on my desk in order for me to study there.

Marcia came up with three disadvantages:

Cost: All of this cleaning is hurting my grades.

Cost: I'm not as stress free as I thought I'd be.

Cost: I'm not getting along with my roommate because she feels she can't relax in our room.

After Marcia reviewed her list of the advantages of procrastinating, she discovered that she wasn't as lazy as she'd convinced herself she was; this realization led to a reduction in her procrastinatory behavior. She no longer believed her own excuses for not doing her work. The time she was spending cleaning could be better used on her studies.

If you conduct your own cost–benefit analysis, you may learn that there are good reasons why you avoid doing something. If this is the case, you may need to reevaluate your goals.

3. *Little steps for big feats.* Most procrastinators tell themselves, "I'll wait until I'm more in the mood." Let's face it: you're never going to *feel* like studying, reading or beginning a term paper. Sometimes you simply have to prime the pump to get yourself going. (Burns, p. 89)

Burns explains that one way to do this is to break a job into steps that can be accomplished bit by bit. Take that 300 pages you have to read this week and spread it over five days. Now take that 60 pages per day and break it into three reading sessions. You could read 20 pages in the morning, 20 in the afternoon, and 20 at night. That doesn't seem as overwhelming, does it?

4. *Tune out negative thoughts.* When you're avoiding a task, it may be because you're feeding yourself unrealistic, negative messages. By writing them down, you have a chance of dispelling them. (Burns, p. 89)

5. *Give yourself credit.* Once you've begun a job you've been avoiding, it's important to give yourself credit as you go along. . . . Too often people discount their accomplishments and focus on what they haven't been able to do.

Burns says that although we often think of rewards as coming from the outside, ultimately all rewards must come from within. Give yourself credit for your accomplishments.

In this chapter, we have seen that it is crucial to prioritize your time while at college. To achieve success, you'll need to be aware of how your time is spent as well as what you can do to be more efficient. The 8–8–8 formula and three-tiered system presented in this chapter will allow you to gain some measure of control over your day—and your semester. Remember, though, that procrastination is the enemy of sound time management practices; be conscious of the ways in which you typically procrastinate, and make the effort to avoid these activities.

DISCUSSION QUESTIONS

1. In the student portraits, students talk about rigorous schedules, budgeting their time, and balancing schoolwork and outside activities. You've been at school for weeks now. How are you balancing the "demanding" college life Ernie mentions? Do you "plan everything out really carefully" like Ann?

2. Describe the academic planning tools you use. How do they compare with the student samples?

3. Which of the antiprocrastination behaviors and habits do you use, if any?

4. Which replacement activities do you typically use when you procrastinate? Why is it important to be aware of these activities?

5. What kinds of things might prevent you from following through if you set up an "academic plan"?

6. Why is planning and prioritizing an important consideration for college students? How does planning relate to course selection?

7. When do you find it most difficult to prioritize tasks? How do you handle these situations?

8. Speaking from your own experience, how would you describe the consequences of failing to plan adequately?

9. How does motivation relate to procrastination?

10. Describe a time when you were very successful in planning and executing a major project or task. What contributed to your success? How can you transfer these skills to your course work?

ACTIVITIES

3.1 Create a semester and weekly schedule. How much time do you have to do course work? Will this be adequate, given what you've learned regarding professors' expectations?

3.2 Exchange your semester schedule with that of one of your classmates. How has your partner broken down large projects/tasks into manageable chunks? Have you done so in your own schedule?

3.3 Choose a study space on campus that meets the criteria outlined in this chapter. Use this new space for at least an hour to do some course work. Were you more efficient in this new study environment? Why or why not? What have you learned about selecting a study space?

3.4 Recall that the experts estimate that the average person lies about 25 times a day. Tune in to your behaviors and thoughts. Keep a lie log for a week, diligently recording each time you tell a lie. Given the three broad categories of lies, can you identify the types of lies you tend to tell? To what extent are your lies feeding into procrastination behavior?

3.5 Take each of the five strategies suggested by David Burns and apply them over the course of the next week: (A) What difficulties arose that you did not expect? Keep a running list. (B) Create a chart of your personal cost–benefit analysis. (C) Choose a paper or project that is due toward the end of the semester and break that "big feat" into "little steps." (D) What negative thoughts crept into your head? Write them down. Discuss the strategies you implemented to "tune out" those thoughts. (E) What kinds of rewards did you use to congratulate yourself for a job well done?

REFERENCES

Britton, B. K., & Tesser, A. (1991). Effects of time-management practices on college grades. *Journal of Educational Psychology, 83*(3), 405–410.

Burns, D. D. (1992, January). Stop putting it off! *Reader's Digest, 140,* 87–90.

Lakein, A. (1973). *How to get control of your time and your life.* New York: P. H. Widden.

Lay, C., & Burns, P. (1991). Intentions and behavior in studying for an examination: The role of trust procrastination and its interaction with optimism. *Journal of Social Behavior and Personality, 6,* 605–617.

Murray, H (1938). *Explorations in personality.* New York: Oxford University Press (p. 373).

Myers, D. G. (2002). *Exploring psychology.* New York: Worth Publishers.

Wesley, J. C. (1994). Effects of ability, high school achievement, and procrastinatory behavior on college performance. *Educational and Psychological Measurement, 54*(2), 404–408.

Developing Metacognitive Skills

T he previous chapters have clearly emphasized that students enter into a transitional period of their lives when they begin college. Experts who study this transitional period identify a variety of issues students have to deal with, such as separation from family and friends, indecision about their majors or future career goals, new relationships, and perhaps even conflicts with family members (Rabinowitz, 1987; Wratcher, 1991). On top of these adjustment issues, this chapter outlines academic adjustment concerns such as developing study habits that are critical to "making the grade" first semester. Naturally, you should be concerned about earning good grades and achieving academically during your first semester, and good study habits will help you to do so; however, as mentioned in the last chapter, good study habits require more than an understanding of *how* to study (how to take notes, how to read, how to manage your time). You must also be motivated and willing to adapt your study habits to each professor's teaching style and expectations. You may sit quietly in one course, taking notes dutifully during daily lectures, whereas you may participate in group exercises every week in another.

To be successful in college, you will need to reexamine how you learn best as well as the various factors that influence your own academic achievement. Many students think they already have college-level study skills when they arrive on campus but soon discover unexpected obstacles and challenges, particularly regarding work done outside of class.

This chapter offers information regarding how students learn: when reading, writing, talking with others, or thinking to themselves. Equally important, this chapter encourages you to reflect on the study methods you currently employ—and to be open to experimenting with new approaches. Attending college involves a process of acculturation. You shouldn't forget everything you ever knew, but the academic demands of college will necessitate that you be open to the idea of trying study strategies that you haven't before.

The study habits inventory that follows, designed by Craig Jones and John Slate, will help you gauge how your current study habits compare with those used by many successful college students.

IN THIS CHAPTER

- How do you learn best?

- What assumptions have you made about learning? What attitudes do you possess in relation to learning?

- Do you have an internal or external locus of control?

- What are some practical approaches to developing metacognitive ability?

- How can writing promote learning?

- How can you read actively and critically?

STUDY HABITS INVENTORY

Craig Jones and John Slate

INSTRUCTIONS: *Read each statement below; fill in the blank spaces to the left of each numbered item using the following key:*

A = *True, I usually study in this way.*
B = *False, I usually do not study in this way.*

Remember, your responses should describe your typical study habits. The inventory will be of value to you only to the extent that you are perfectly honest in answering the questions.

_____ 1. I study most subjects with the idea of remembering the material only until the test is over.

_____ 2. I try to write down everything my instructor says, as close to word-for-word as possible.

_____ 3. If I am sure I will remember something, I do not write it in my notes even if it seems to be important.

_____ 4. I try to complete assigned readings before my instructor discusses them in class.

_____ 5. I sometimes skip classes, especially when attendance is not required.

_____ 6. When sitting in my classes, I have a tendency to daydream about other things.

_____ 7. When taking notes in class, I simply try to get everything down so that I do not have to take the time to think about what the material means.

_____ 8. When taking notes in class, I abbreviate words and jot down phrases rather than complete sentences.

_____ 9. I tend to include a lot of irrelevant or unimportant information in my notes.

_____ 10. When I take notes, I try to follow an outline or some other type of organized format.

_____ 11. I take notes on odd, loose slips of paper instead of in a notebook.

_____ 12. I keep the notes for all my classes in the same notebook.

_____ 13. As soon as possible after class, I recopy my lecture notes.

_____ 14. Except for important quotations and the definitions of technical terms, I copy my notes in my own words rather than the exact words used by my instructor or my textbook.

_____ 15. When I have difficulty with my work, I do not hesitate to seek help from my instructor.

_____ 16. I put my lecture notes away after an exam and never look at them again.

_____ 17. I tape-record lectures instead of taking notes.

_____ 18. I have a definite, although reasonably flexible, study schedule with times for studying specific subjects.

_____ 19. I spend too much time on loafing, movies, dates, and so forth that I should be spending on my course work.

_____ 20. I spend too much time on some subjects and not enough on others.

_____ 21. My study periods are too short for me to get "warmed up" and really concentrate on studying.

_____ 22. I usually write reports several days before they are due, so that I can correct them if necessary.

_____ 23. I frequently do not get enough sleep and feel sluggish in class or when studying.

_____ 24. I often do not have reports ready on time, or they are done poorly if I am forced to have them in on time.

_____ 25. I do most of my reviewing for a test the night before the examination.

_____ 26. I try to space my study periods so that I do not become too tired while studying.

_____ 27. I stick to my study schedule except for very good reasons.

_____ 28. My study time is interrupted frequently by telephone calls, visitors, and other distractions.

_____ 29. I have trouble settling down to work and do not begin studying as soon as I sit down.

_____ 30. I have to wait for the mood to strike me before attempting to study.

_____ 31. I frequently get up, write notes to friends, or look at other people when I should be studying.

_____ 32. I have a tendency to doodle or daydream when I am trying to study.

_____ 33. I often study with a radio or stereo playing, or with other people talking in the same room.

_____ 34. I often sit down to study only to find that I do not have the necessary books, notes, or other materials.

_____ 35. I read by indirect (diffused) light rather than by direct light.

_____ 36. To help stay awake while studying, I frequently drink a lot of coffee or other beverages that are high in caffeine.

_____ 37. I often try to make schoolwork more enjoyable by having a beer while studying.

_____ 38. I make a preliminary survey by skimming a chapter before reading it in detail.

_____ 39. I use the headings to make an outline of a chapter before I begin to read it.

_____ 40. Before reading a chapter, I jot down a few questions and a list of key terms to focus my attention while reading.

_____ 41. I pause at logical breaks in my reading, such as the end of a section or chapter, and recite to myself the principle ideas in that section.

_____ 42. Sometimes I discover that I have "read" several pages without knowing what was on them.

_____ 43. I take notes after I have completed a reading assignment rather than take notes as I go along.

_____ 44. I look up in a dictionary the meanings of words that I do not understand.

_____ 45. I tend to skip over the boxes, tables, and graphs in a reading assignment.

_____ 46. In studying a textbook, I try to memorize the exact words in the text.

_____ 47. Sometimes I make simple charts or diagrams to show how the facts I am learning are related to each other.

_____ 48. I try to break large amounts of information into small clusters that can be studied separately.

_____ 49. I work out personal examples to illustrate general principles or rules that I have learned.

_____ 50. I use the facts I learned in one course to help me understand the material in another course.

_____ 51. I practice using new words by putting them into meaningful sentences.

_____ 52. I use the facts learned in school to help me understand events outside of school.

_____ 53. I try to think critically about new material and not simply accept everything I read.

_____ 54. I frequently test myself to see if I have learned the material I am studying.

_____ 55. I keep a special indexed notebook or card system for recording new words and their meanings.

_____ 56. I review frequently.

_____ 57. I try to do some "over learning," working beyond the point of immediate recall.

_____ 58. I review previous work before beginning work on an advanced assignment.

_____ 59. If I plan to study with friends, I do not study by myself ahead of time.

_____ 60. Whenever possible, I use the workbook that accompanies a textbook.

_____ 61. I often read too slowly to complete reading assignments on time.

_____ 62. I have to reread material several times before I get the meaning of it.

_____ 63. I have trouble picking out the important points in the material I read.

SCORING: *When you've finished, match your responses to those in the key below. Give yourself one point for each matched item. Your score will range between 0 and 63. The raw score you receive divided by 63 indicates the percentage of college-level study skills you are currently using. If, for example, your score is 31, you are using roughly 50 percent of the study habits that will make you successful in college. This tells you that there is ample room for improvement; you are operating at only half capacity.*

ANSWER KEY

1. B	10. A	19. B	28. B	37. B	46. B	55. A
2. B	11. B	20. B	29. B	38. A	47. A	56. A
3. B	12. A	21. B	30. B	39. A	48. A	57. A
4. A	13. A	22. A	31. B	40. A	49. A	58. A
5. B	14. A	23. B	32. B	41. A	50. A	59. B
6. B	15. A	24. B	33. B	42. B	51. A	60. A
7. B	16. B	25. B	34. B	43. B	52. A	61. B
8. A	17. B	26. A	35. A	44. A	53. A	62. B
9. B	18. A	27. A	36. B	45. B	54. A	63. B

Used with permission of Drs. Craig H. Jones and John R. Slate.

WHY SHOULD I CHANGE?

You might be asking: "Why should I change my study habits? I'm in college; I already know how to study." Take the skill of memorization, for instance. Many students coming out of high school have relied solely on this method to "learn" material for their classes. This method may have resulted in a fair grade point average (GPA) in high school, but employing this strategy to prepare for college-level material will not work, because professors have different expectations. Because the application of high school study skills, such as memorization, will not yield the same results in a college environment as they did in high school, it is not uncommon for college personnel to hear from first-year students, "I don't understand why I received a C on that test. I always got As and Bs in high school" or "I have always been a good writer. I don't understand why I'm having so much trouble in my composition class." Researchers attempt to explain such perspectives of first-year college students.

Some researchers who have examined effective methods of studying in college are aware that the application of study skills in college should be a response to the differing types of requirements of college courses (Thomas, Bol, & Warkentin, 1991). This kind of research indicates that course features between high school and college differ greatly in workload, degree of cognitive challenge, and need for self-direction. As opposed to high school, where teachers helped students adapt to the different demands of each class—a **teacher-directed environment**—in college, students are expected to adapt to such variability on their own—in a **student-directed environment**. In this student-directed environment, you will now be expected to identify "the most important information" in textbooks or "what will be on the test." Your professors are not likely to approach you if they suspect that you are having difficulty with material, particularly if the roots of your difficulties lie in the area of study skills (Wratcher, 1991). Consequently, in order to achieve academically, you must either already have or quickly develop the appropriate study skills needed to respond to the change in the learning environment from high school to college.

A wide range of skills and strategies have been identified as the study skills needed for "making the grade" in college. Some researchers describe the necessary study skills as reading, writing, and finding and organizing information (Reynolds & Werner, 1994). Others define time management, listening, note taking, test taking, problem solving, and critical thinking as the necessary skills for college achievement (Anderson & Anderson, 1992). Clearly, a vast repertoire of skills is needed for college success, so what this means for you is that you will have to figure out which you possess and which need honing.

Academic success in college largely depends on your capacity to self-reflect, to become aware of and able to control your own study habits. Regulation of study behaviors is commonly called **metacognition**. Metacognitive strategies allow students to plan, monitor, evaluate, and revise learning strategies whenever needed in studying and learning new materials. Students with the ability to self-regulate have at least four things in common. They set goals; develop and adapt diverse methods to strive toward those goals; are motivationally engaged in the process; and are metacognitively aware of the learning decisions, processes, and products that those processes create (Hadwin & Winne, 1996; Turner, 1992; White & Kitchen, 1991).

How can you become metacognitively aware? Well, some type of study skills training is a start, but you'll also need to consider your current attitude(s) toward learning. Students may know what effective study skills are, may make an effort to acquire those study skills, and may even achieve competency in the area of study skills after having received study skills training. However, for study skills to have an effect on academic achievement, students must *use* the study skills that have been taught to them. If students have developed good study skills, what would prevent them from using their skills, especially if they know doing so will help them earn higher grades?

Experts question student utilization of newly learned study skills. They reason that even if students do learn more effective study skills, whether they will utilize these skills depends, to a large degree, on their perception of whether the use of these skills will make a difference (Jones, Slate, & Marini, 1995). Students will say things like, "I never liked to read or was very good at it. I can't see how using this new type of outlining is going to change that." Or students will say, "Sure, I know I should take notes when I read, but I just can't picture myself taking the time to do it. What difference will it make, anyhow?" Internalizing these beliefs essentially gives students permission to avoid the hard work of changing their old study habits.

For many first-year students, the thought of adding study skills training that challenges them to change their habits seems a burden. What students don't often consider is that ineffective study strategies often take much longer to implement and yield inconsistent or poor results. Taking the time to learn college-level study strategies can literally be a time saver. The idea that changing study habits is a waste of time is just one of the faulty internalized beliefs that impact whether students are willing to change the way they study. There are others, which we discuss next.

STUDENT ATTITUDES TOWARD LEARNING

As mentioned, research indicates that teaching first-year students specific study strategies is a worthwhile goal, because better study habits in college lead to higher achievement. You may now be convinced that changing your high school study habits is a worthwhile endeavor. Many students do come to the realization that their habits must change and become open to learning new strategies. Unfortunately, oftentimes they realize this only after their high school study habits fail them. As discussed, of further concern is that once students learn college-level study strategies, not all students will use them.

Whether students use new strategies depends on their attitudes. Researchers point out that in order for students to use their new study skills, the attitudes that influence their use need to be addressed (Jones et al., 1995). In other words, reflecting upon your attitudes toward learning might be of equal importance to learning new college-level study skills. Two particular attitudes have been found to influence strongly whether you will use study skills you have been taught: your locus of control and your attitude toward intelligence.

What Is Your Locus of Control?

Locus of control involves a generalized expectancy that people hold regarding the degree to which they control their fate (Jones, Slate, Marini, & Dewater, 1993). This expectancy is an attitude that influences students' use of academic skills. Some people believe that what happens to them is largely determined by personal effort, ability, and initiative whereas others believe outcomes are largely determined by other people, social structures, luck, or fate. People with an **internal locus of control** feel that they have a reasonable amount of control over their outcomes. People with an **external locus of control** feel that their fate is largely beyond their control. According to Lefcourt (1982), whether people believe that they can determine their own fates, within limits, is of critical importance to the way they cope with stress and engage in challenges.

Oftentimes, first-year students see college as novel, ambiguous, and, well, stressful (Cone & Owens, 1991). Dealing with the anxiety of social and academic adjustment issues is not easy. Locus of control can affect the way students adjust to the stresses and challenges of the first semester. If students don't see that they can control their personal fate within their new surroundings, they can begin to feel alienated from the scholarly environment. Not only can locus of control influence adjustment to stress; it can also affect whether students get involved in the pursuit of achievement (Lefcourt, 1982).

Locus of control relates here to delayed gratification. For students, the future value of their efforts is not always obvious—what student hasn't wanted to close the textbook and head outside with friends? Class work is often repetitive and may interfere with more enjoyable activities. College is a place that offers the opportunity for achievement and it requires a degree of self-management, conscious effort, and sacrifice in order to attain future goals. For people who doubt the potential of their efforts, sacrifice is improbable (Lefcourt, 1982).

Locus of control is a complex concept. Whether you have an internal or external locus of control will affect the likelihood of your using college-level study skills. Some studies show that locus of control is the most powerful predictor of whether you will use new study skills. External and internal students differ primarily in terms of both motivation to study and their ability to concentrate on academic work: "Students with an external locus of control were not only less likely to study than students with an internal locus of control, but were also more likely to be distracted from studying once they had begun" (Lefcourt, 1982, p. 60). The results of these studies suggest that it is critical for you to look at the motivational and attitudinal variables that affect your utilization of study skills. If you have an external locus of control, you will need to make a conscious effort to apply the new skills you have learned.

Measure your locus of control with the Trice Academic Locus of Control Scale

As we have discussed, locus of control refers to the degree to which people feel they control their own fate—an attitude that refers to a generalized expectancy about the extent to which reinforcements are under internal or external control. If individuals believe events are controlled by luck, fate, chance, or powerful others, they are called externals (external locus of control), as opposed to internals (internal locus of control), individuals who believe an event is contingent upon their own behavior.

Locus of control plays a mediating role in determining whether students get involved in the pursuit of achievement. A significant correlation has been found between locus of control and GPA (see Exhibit 4.1). By completing the Trice Academic Locus of Control Scale, you will see how your locus of control correlates with your GPA.

EXHIBIT 4.1	Correlation between locus of control and GPA.

Internal Locus of Control		External Locus of Control
0	14	28
GPA	GPA	GPA
4.0	2.0	0.0

TRICE ACADEMIC LOCUS OF CONTROL SCALE

INSTRUCTIONS: *Read each statement below; fill in the blank spaces to the left of each numbered item with an "F" for False or a "T" for True.*

_____ 1. College grades most often reflect the effort you put into classes.

_____ 2. I came to college because it was expected of me.

_____ 3. I have largely determined my own career goals.

_____ 4. Some people have a knack for writing, whereas others will never write well no matter how hard they try.

_____ 5. At least once, I have taken a course because it was easy to get a good grade.

_____ 6. Professors sometimes make an early impression of you and then no matter what you do, you cannot change that impression.

_____ 7. There are some subjects in which I could never do well.

_____ 8. Some students, such as student leaders and athletes, get free rides in college classes.

_____ 9. I sometimes feel that there is nothing I can do to improve my situation.

_____ 10. I never feel really hopeless; there is always something I can do to improve my situation.

_____ 11. I would never allow social activities to affect my studies.

_____ 12. There are many more important things for me than getting good grades.

_____ 13. Studying every day is important.

_____ 14. For some courses it is not important to go to class.

_____ 15. I consider myself highly motivated to achieve success in life.

_____ 16. I am a good writer.

_____ 17. Doing work on time is always important to me.

_____ 18. What I learn is more determined by college and course requirements than by what I want to learn.

_____ 19. I have been known to spend a lot of time making decisions that others do not take seriously.

_____ 20. I am easily distracted.

_____ 21. I can be easily talked out of studying.

_____ 22. I get depressed sometimes and then there is no way I can accomplish what I know I should be doing.

_____ 23. Things will probably go wrong for me some time in the near future.

_____ 24. I keep changing my mind about my career goals.

_____ 25. I feel I will someday make a real contribution to the world if I work hard at it.

_____ 26. There has been at least one instance in school in which social activity impaired my academic performance.

_____ 27. I would like to graduate from college, but there are more important things in my life.

_____ 28. I plan well and I stick to my plans

SCORING: *When you've finished, match your responses to those in the key below. Give yourself one point for each matched item. Your score will range between 0 and 28. As indicated above, the scores are significantly correlated with GPA. Low scores are associated with higher GPAs and high scores are associated with lower GPAs.*

ANSWER KEY

1. F	8. T	15. F	22. T
2. T	9. T	16. F	23. T
3. F	10. F	17. F	24. T
4. T	11. F	18. T	25. F
5. T	12. T	19. F	26. T
6. T	13. F	20. T	27. T
7. T	14. T	21. T	28. F

Trice, A. D. An academic locus of control scale for college students. *Perceptual and Motor Skills,* 1985, 1043-1046.
© Perceptual and Motor Skills 1985. Used with permission.

Consider Your Attitude Toward Intelligence

Carol Dweck and Ellen Leggett (1988) propose that your **attitude toward intelligence** is another reliable indicator of your use of academic skills. They argue that people hold one of two basic viewpoints of intelligence: an entity view or an incremental view. People who hold an *entity view* believe that intelligence is a fixed, single ability. Thus, ability, not effort, is the key factor that determines performance. People who hold an *incremental view* believe that intelligence involves a set of skills that can be improved through effort.

Building on the work of Dweck and Leggett, other researchers have found that college students with an incremental view of intelligence tend to work harder and thus exhibit stronger use of study skills, compared with students with an entity view of intelligence (Jones et al., 1993). The research indicates that students with an incremental view engage in more positive academic behaviors than do students with an entity view. More specifically, Jones et al. (1993) found that, compared with students with an entity view, students with an incremental view invest a greater effort in their education. They are more likely to complete reading and written assignments ahead of time, are less likely to engage in rote memorization, and are less likely to daydream in class (Jones et al., 1993).

There Are Multiple Theories of Intelligence

Naturally, at some point, when students think about their ability to be successful in college, they ask themselves, "Am I smart enough to be here?" Students' beliefs regarding the nature and strength of their academic abilities will influence whether they will use new study skills. You've heard students say things like, "I was born bad at math. No amount of tutoring is going to fix that." Such students possess an entity view of intelligence, causing them to react to learning challenges by claiming that their problems are unsolvable, preventing them from seeking to improve by implementing new skills. This can also work in the reverse—that is, for students who have been successful and would not likely question their abilities.

Students who perceive themselves as strong academically face the traditional issues of college adjustment, and they too might be faced with having to form new learning strategies (Wratcher, 1991). A history of academic success affects the way talented students react to difficulty or failure in college. For example, because talented students are unaccustomed to dealing with academic difficulties, it takes them longer to recognize patterns of academic trouble and to seek assistance. In approaching their studies, talented students tend to be rigid in learning approaches and strategies and may possess unrealistic academic goals (Wratcher, 1991). Remember Colleen from Chapter One? Think about how it wasn't until subpar performance on two exams that she was able to begin to break through the rigidity of the index card learning approach. This can be a painful way to learn, but Colleen was able to take something positive from the experience.

The question remains, "Are you smart enough to be here?" The answer is, "That depends." In college, there's a difference between "being intelligent" and "doing intelligent." You could have the highest IQ on campus, but if you are not using your smarts, it won't make a difference; again, this is what distinguishes an entity view of intelligence from an incremental view of intelligence. Take two students of equal ability. One procrastinates and avoids schoolwork whereas the other is diligent and hardworking. Who will be viewed as more intelligent?

In college, there's a difference between "being intelligent" and "doing intelligent."

There is a perennial debate among scholars over what constitutes or defines intelligence. In the 1960s, personality characteristics and attitudes as they relate to academic achievement and intelligence began to receive attention. This awareness led educators to begin to question our culture's traditional views of intelligence.

Howard Gardner's (1983) **theory of multiple intelligences (MI theory)** challenges the idea that intelligence is a single capacity that "equips" a person to deal with various situations. Gardner would likely challenge the entity view of intelligence. He argues that people use at least seven autonomous intellectual capacities with their own distinctive ways of thinking. He suggests that people use the *seven intelligences,*

Maria: "For me as a person, it would make me more comfortable to know I have a social environment to make me more confident in my schoolwork, 'cause I'm not always confident in what I can produce. I think that holds true for a lot of people. You have to have your confidence in either one thing or another, and, if it's your academics, your social environment can maybe produce around that, or academics can produce around your social."

which he identifies as linguistic, musical, logical–mathematical, spatial, bodily–kinesthetic, interpersonal, and intrapersonal, to approach problems and create products. According to Gardner:

A human intellectual competence must entail a set of skills of problem solving—enabling an individual to resolve genuine problems or difficulties that he or she encounters and, when appropriate, to create an effective product—and must also entail the potential for finding or creating problems—thereby laying the groundwork for the acquisition of new knowledge. (p. 61)

To enforce his point, Gardner provides an example of a 12-year-old male Puluwat in the Caroline Islands who has mastered sailing. Under the tutelage of master navigators, the boy learns to combine the knowledge of sailing, stars, and geography in order to find his way around hundreds of islands. The boy exhibits a high level of competence in a challenging field and should, Gardner argues, be viewed as exhibiting intelligent behavior, or "doing intelligent."

The research on student achievement, along with Gardner's (1983) theory of multiple intelligences, has received a great deal of attention in the field of education and has sparked endless debate about the factors that contribute to and predict student achievement. It seems apparent from this research that besides using the traditional modes of standardized tests of intelligence and aptitude to predict academic achievement, other factors should be considered. Nevertheless, most institutions of higher education still rely on the traditional admissions credentials of high school grades and SAT scores in spite of research that suggests attitudinal and personality factors may be additional reliable criteria for predicting academic achievement. Again, take those two students of equal ability. Their admissions credentials—SAT scores and high school grades—are virtually identical. One can't get motivated to do the required work, whereas the other has established a daily routine for studying. In this case, who is more likely to achieve academically in college?

Another person who questions how we traditionally look at intelligence is Daniel Goleman (1995). He questions the ways in which intelligence is quantified in our culture, in particular through a shift in interest from intelligence quotient to **emotional intelligence.** Emotional intelligence includes qualities that those who are high achievers share: self-awareness, impulse control, persistence, and self-motivation. A person's belief system, for instance, affects her or his achievement. Goleman's work is based on that of the Stanford psychologist Albert Bandura, who offered insight into a concept called self-efficacy. **Self-efficacy** is the belief that you are capable of producing desired results, such as mastering new skills and achieving personal goals. Simply put, "If you believe you can do it, you can." Think about situations in which you feel confident and how you might act compared with situations in which you feel, well, insecure. The idea of self-efficacy is directly related to what study skills educators say regarding students' beliefs about their own academic abilities, including the relationship between students' loci of control and their study habits (Jones et al., 1993). If you believe the new study habits you have learned will produce desired results, and you recognize this as a result of your own efforts, you will more likely continue to use those new strategies and feel confident about doing so.

APPROACHES TO LEARNING

Even those students with the most positive attitude toward learning can benefit from thinking more critically about how they learn. The remainder of this chapter explores various approaches to learning that employ metacognition, reflecting on the ways you come to understand.

As we discussed in Chapter One, it is easy to remain entrenched in old habits, in old ways of thinking and learning. Remember how Friedman and Lipshitz (1992) called this "stuckness" **automatic thinking?** They explain that students sometimes are immobilized when it comes to learning new information because of past experiences. Learning from experience, which seems to be a natural activity, is a critical skill for individuals and organizations. Experiential learning, however, results in behavior that tends to occur automatically rather than from conscious thought. Friedman and Lipshitz (1992) note that the advantage of automatic thinking can become a disadvantage when in the face of change or uncertainty. They argue that automatic thinking leads people to rely on what they already know and contributes to the tendency to ignore critical information, and rely on standard behavior repertoires when change is required. That is, people will continue to do what they feel most comfortable doing even if it isn't working for them; they resist change. Aside from experiential learning, other types of learning require switching to a more conscious reflective mode, and researchers argue that people resist switching to this mode when it's needed the most. This conscious reflective mode is metacognition.

Let's take these concepts and apply them to your utilization of new study strategies. You are stuck in your old study habits that you learned from experience in high school. For four years those habits served you well. You graduated from high school with a B average. Without thinking about it much, you "automatically" apply those strategies when you get to college. You don't even think about it. Why would you? Your ways always worked in the past, but now you are faced with change and uncertainty. Your automatic thinking causes you to ignore critical information. Like Colleen in Chapter One, you don't get great results using your study habits from high school, but you don't bother to look at how you might change your ways to adapt to the demands of college. You can't move out of your comfort zone, but you have to because you aren't happy with your grades. To understand how your study habits affect your grades, you need to enter into that reflective mode of thinking. One way to start is by considering your learning style.

Identify Your Learning Style(s)

Study strategies are often taught using a "one size fits all" approach. In many instances, students are taught one particular way of taking notes, and the assumption is that every person will benefit from applying that particular note-taking technique. **Learning styles theory**, on the other hand, addresses the ways in which a person learns best and tailors approaches to learning and studying based on the individual. Study experts such as Reynolds and Werner (1994) advocate for an approach that is "learner-centered, where individuals develop personal ways of learning which can be called learning style characteristics. This pattern of personality and environmental factors related to how one learns is called 'learning style'" (p. 272). For some students, a learner-centered approach is a worthwhile pursuit, and students need to take the time to develop their own personal ways of learning. Students usually have a preferred way of learning new material, via one or more of several sensory modalities, including auditory, visual, and tactile/kinesthetic. Simply put, people process information using their ears, their eyes, and their sense of touch.

Auditory learners use their ears as the primary mode for learning. They are most likely to remember what they hear and what they say. If they find something difficult to understand, they want to talk it through. Professors may notice that auditory learners tend not to take as many notes in class as other students do. Auditory learners have a keen ability to remember things without writing them down. When they want to remember something, they use verbal rehearsal techniques. That is, they go over concepts by saying them aloud, sometimes several times, because the oral repetition will implant the information in their minds. These are the students who get heavily involved in class discussions. On the downside, auditory processors may get easily distracted because they attend to all of the sounds around them. They are uncomfortable when forced to work quietly at their desks for an extended period of time or study in a quiet room (Guild & Garger, 1986).

Visual learners want to see a picture; they want to actually see the words written down. For example, a visual learner would find handouts, overheads, and PowerPoint slides very helpful in the classroom. These learners tune in to the physical environment. They like to organize their own materials and work spaces. They prefer illustrations, diagrams, and charts to help them understand and remember information. They tend to review and study material by reading over their notes and recopying and reorganizing them in outline form (Guild & Garger, 1986).

Tactile/kinesthetic learners prefer learning when they are physically involved in what they are studying. These learners want to act out a situation, create a product, or work on a project. They understand and remember best when they physically do something. They may take lots of notes to keep their hands busy, but they may avoid rereading the notes. They learn a new skill by actually trying it, experimenting, and practicing. They learn concepts in history by simulating experiences in the classroom. They become interested in poetry by becoming physically involved in the thoughts expressed. Many of these learners want to be as active as possible during the learning experience (Guild & Garger, 1986).

Mixed modality learners are able to function in more than one modality. Students with mixed modality strengths often have a better chance of success than do those with a single modality strength, because they are able to process information in whatever way it is presented (Guild & Garger, 1986).

You may have arrived at college favoring one of the three primary learning styles (auditory, visual, tactile/kinesthetic). Because study experts say that you have a better chance at success if you are a mixed modality learner, you should identify your preferred style and work on developing the other modes.

Many students complain, for instance, that they have trouble learning in classes that rely primarily on PowerPoint presentations for instruction. Part of the problem is likely that these students are not visual processors but, rather, auditory or tactile/kinesthetic processors. They may be yearning for some class discussion or perhaps group exercises. So what should such students do about the situation? Unfortunately, students often have little or no control over the way in which information is presented, which is precisely why mixed modality learners have a better chance of success—they are able to process information no matter how it is presented. Your challenge is to identify your preferred style and work on strengthening the modes with which you are least comfortable. Because you often have little influence over the ways your professors choose to teach, you should enhance the extent to which you can learn in various contexts. To do so, you should formulate study strategies that tap into all three learning modalities. The remaining chapters will help you with this endeavor.

Writing Can Help You Better Understand How You Learn

Writing is a metacognitive activity. Much can be learned about how you think through the process of writing. In fact, although many students say that they'd like to learn how to be a better writer, fewer students fully utilize writing as a learning tool. Writing isn't just a way for you to demonstrate what you know, it is also a way to discover and experiment with ideas, to arrive at an understanding. This view of writing suggests that you needn't have things all figured out when you sit down at your blank computer screen or with pen and paper. Viewing writing as a means of discovery means that you don't always know where your sentences will take you.

> ### Make It Personal
>
> Do you consider writing as an opportunity for learning or as a demonstration of what you already "know"?

Imagine, for example, that you decided to write a paper about the Fox television show *The Simpsons*. You thought that you would focus on Homer and Marge as parents. That would be your topic. Now you need to have something to say about that topic: what do you think of these animated parents? This idea will be your working thesis, maybe something like: "Homer and Marge Simpson are terrible parents." Simple enough. You begin to brainstorm, writing down what you can remember about Homer and Marge as parents. You do your best to remember specific episodes and particular events. You are using writing to remember, record, and build upon itself.

When you look at what you've come up with, though, you discover that most of your examples don't illustrate the point you originally thought you'd make. It turns out that the events you've been able to recall mainly illustrate that Homer and Marge are typical parents, doing their best and making mistakes along the way. Now what?

Should you give up and select another topic? The most logical thing to do would be to revise your working thesis so that it conforms to your "findings," the ideas you've generated through brainstorming. This is an example of how writing—in coordination with reflective thinking—can lead you to think differently. Everything isn't already in your head waiting to be dumped onto 8½-by-11-inch sheets of paper.

The goal of a **reflective journal**, in fact, is to think through ideas by writing about them—to figure things out by putting pen to paper or fingertip to keyboard. Journals allow "students and teachers [to] work together through written language to understand disciplinary content—its problems and its possibilities, and its value, usefulness, and connections to other disciplines and other situations" (Gardner & Fulwiler, 1999, p. vi). The act of keeping a reflective journal involves making regular entries and collecting them together to illustrate your thinking over a period of time—typically a semester. These entries might reveal a linear thought process, but they might also reflect back on earlier entries to challenge, extend, or complicate ideas. A journal is not a notebook. It is not a summary of what happened in class or a collection of notes regarding course readings. Professors typically encourage students to use journals to question, disagree, argue, complicate, extend, connect, evaluate, or identify the impact of discussions or readings.

Make It Personal

How could you use a journal in one of your classes this semester?

Some professors *require* the use of a journal, some *recommend* keeping a journal, and others say nothing about journals at all. Because journals are a way for you to be actively involved in a course, you might consider putting some effort into keeping a journal regardless of whether it is required or recommended. Doing so will help you engage with what you are learning on a personal level, giving you a safe space to ask questions and attempt answers on a regular basis.

The collection of entries that comprise a journal will likely indicate what you feel and think about discussions you had in class, what you've read in and outside of class, campus-sponsored or promoted events you've attended, and other such reflective opportunities. If the journal is required, your professor may offer prompts to which your entries are expected to respond. Your professor may even suggest that you respond to ideas you voiced earlier, in previous entries; these responses have the potential to show you how your thinking changes over time. You might consider discussing what you believe happened between the two entries that caused you to see things differently (if indeed you do). If keeping a journal is your own choice, you can decide on your own prompts, connecting what you are learning to your own personal experience.

If a journal is required, you will likely be asked to bring your journal with you to at least some class meetings. You may be asked to use the journal in class, to do things such as read part of an entry to the class, refer to the journal as you take a quiz, or compose a new entry.

Portfolio Development as a Metacognitive Activity

Portfolios, collections of student work, emphasize metacognition, requiring those who keep a portfolio to consider what it will include, to make decisions regarding content, organization, and scope, for example. As with journals, portfolios may be required, recommended, or not mentioned by your professors. Depending on the situation, a portfolio can consist of writing, artwork, videotaped presentations, PowerPoint slides, sample databases, websites, and other artifacts. A portfolio might reveal things about your experiences in a course—or in your entire college experience.

Nedra Reynolds (2000), a rhetoric and composition scholar, explains the benefits of writing portfolios, benefits that would certainly apply to other types of portfolios as well: "Through reflective learning, you can focus on your patterns, habits, and preferences as a student and a writer; learn to repeat what works well for you; and develop strategies for addressing or overcoming the parts of writing that frustrate or puzzle you" (p. 1). Although reflection is inherent in the process of compiling a portfolio, the readers of your portfolio may also want some measure of this reflection, perhaps in the form of a letter, videotaped or audiotaped explanation, painting, or photograph—something that shows what you've learned through putting the portfolio together.

What, for example, made you decide to include those particular artifacts? Why have you arranged them in the order you have? What did you learn about your audience or viewer as you reworked these pieces, and how did you accommodate your audience's/viewers' needs? If you are asked to include a reflective component in your portfolio, you should welcome the opportunity to stand back from your work and look at what you've produced.

Read Actively to Employ Multiple Learning Modalities

Like many students, you have probably experienced something similar to the following scenario: When Antonio sits down to read, he reads several pages, and nothing sinks in at all. He quickly becomes frustrated and gives up on the reading. He then goes to class feeling like a fraud, praying that the professor won't notice that he didn't do the reading. "Someone else will surely answer the questions," he thinks, "and I'll be able to just hide in the background." Antonio also hopes his professor will cover what he was supposed to read during the lecture, so he'll be able to rely on his class notes for the test. This strategy of avoidance catches up with him eventually, because the primary vehicle for learning new material in college, aside from classroom instruction, is reading. Antonio soon discovers that questions on the exam were largely derived from his textbook, and that class lectures were designed as a backdrop for discussing what he was already supposed to know. The lectures didn't go into nearly as much depth as his textbook. Antonio finds that avoiding reading is significantly affecting his test grades. In addition, it is affecting his class participation grade.

Antonio decides that, for the next test, he is really going to try to make the effort. He looks at the syllabus, and for this class he finds that he has to read about 350 pages per week. By applying the academic goal-setting strategy and breaking up the reading into more manageable increments, that comes to about 50 pages a day. "No problem," he thinks. With highlighter in hand, Antonio begins to read the first 50 pages. For the first few pages, things seem to be going well. After some time has passed, however, he realizes it's happening again. Things just aren't sinking in, and as he looks down at the page he's just read, he realizes that half the page is now hot pink from all of the highlighting he's done. On the bright side, Antonio does remember what he's read from the first three pages. The rest, however, is a blur, and he is a full 20 pages into the 50 he set out to read. Looking at the clock, he sees that an hour has passed. How is he going to finish this reading assignment? Frustration and anxiety build. He doesn't know what to do. He feels like such a slow reader.

What could be happening when you are reading is that you are on autopilot.

Like Antonio, what could be happening to you when you are reading is that you are on autopilot. Most students have been reading since their early years in elementary school. It is such an overlearned activity that it is done automatically. To read for comprehension, you need to reflect on what you are reading. Instead of doing so, however, many students reach for the highlighter.

Using a highlighter may make you feel better. You can unwittingly fool yourself into believing that you are doing something productive about your comprehension. After highlighting, you can visually track your passage through a text—you can see that you have proceeded through the chapter. Unfortunately, using a highlighter tends to contribute to passive reading. You could highlight a book while you are stretched out on your bed, but you'll merely end up back on autopilot, swiping different colored ink over lines of text.

Think for a minute about what the inside of a textbook looks like. Grab a textbook and check it out. Notice the format and structure. The main headings and subheadings are in bold print. Content vocabulary words are in italics and/or bold. There are likely shaded boxes with graphic organizers and important information. What do you know—the textbook authors have already done the highlighting for you! If you are highlighting text beyond what they have, chances are you are focusing on the information at a factual level. You are reading for understanding and memorizing definitions. As we have already discussed, learning at college goes beyond testing for factual recall of information.

One general approach to textbook reading will assist students of all learning styles. This approach—**active reading**—crosses over all three learning modalities, which will support your retention of the material. There is no one fixed approach to active reading. The process could go something like this. Begin by reading a passage or paragraph. Use imagery, a visual processing activity, in an attempt to picture what you are reading. To monitor your comprehension—in order to remain in a reflective-thinking mode rather than an automatic-thinking mode—then summarize the passage in your own words, and question yourself about your level of understanding (auditory processing). In other words, have an ongoing dialogue with the text. Think about acting as an interpreter of textual information. Imagine that you have to translate the information from "text" language into "student" language. Record your translation. Verify the information from another source; consider the questions your teacher might ask regarding the passage and record those questions (tactile/kinesthetic processing). Change the main headings/topics into questions. The key here is to read purposefully. You should learn to read skill-fully for such purposes as these:

1. to get the main idea
2. to get the important details
3. to answer a specific question
4. to evaluate what you are reading
5. to apply what you are reading

Not only will applying what you've read take your metacognitive processing to a deeper level and improve your comprehension, but it also will serve you well on tests and quizzes by increasing your memory retention. Next, look for examples in the textbook that the authors use to illustrate key concepts. Record them. You may also generate your own examples to illustrate these concepts in the text. This activity will help build the information into your own **schema**. In other words, connect the new information you are learning to what you already know. Finally, use margin notes to record your understanding of the textual information, a strategy called text annotation, covered in more detail later in this chapter.

It is possible to become a better reader. You may feel that this active-reading approach won't save you any time at all. You may be thinking to yourself, "Why would I do this? I'm already a slow reader and this is going to make a bad situation worse." Granted, this approach may initially take a little longer, but, with practice, active reading will become a more efficient way to read. Why? For one thing, active reading yields better comprehension. You may have been reading a little faster before, but what's the point if you weren't remembering what you were reading? Reading more effectively and efficiently means accomplishing more in less time; enhanced learning; and, likely, increased class participation and retention of information.

Think of active reading this way: reading is like running; both require periodic training and practice. As you work on becoming a more effective and efficient reader, you will at times feel discouraged, but don't quit. Work hard and steadily as if training for a marathon. At first, with no practice, you may only be able to run 1 mile without getting fatigued, but with daily practice, you build up to 5 miles, then 10. Similarly, you may only be able to read a few pages actively without getting fatigued. Like the dedicated runner, you persist, keep at it every day, and eventually build up your endurance. You will eventually become a good reader. Good readers read for a purpose, read thought units rather than words, have many reading rates, evaluate what they read, have a good vocabulary, read varied materials, and enjoy reading.

There are things that you can do to improve your reading speed and comprehension. You might try reading at the same times every day. Doing so trains your mind to be in thinking mode at those times, which cuts down on the time it takes you to become engaged. You should also consider the environment in which you read: avoid places where there are continued distractions, and be sure the area is properly lit. Although students often think in terms of slow readers and fast readers, effective readers are able to alter the rate at which they read and are conscious of this rate. It is necessary in particular contexts and situations to read slowly—for example, in reading Shakespeare for the first time. Reading such a text at an increased rate would result in little comprehension taking place. Effective readers also strive to improve their own vocabulary. As you come across words you don't know, or don't understand in a particular context, take the appropriate opportunity to discover what the words mean. You might even consider keeping a word journal, in which you write "new" words and their corresponding definitions. This kinesthetic exercise should help you develop your vocabulary more quickly.

Reading effectively means having an adequate level of comprehension. Just as you should take the time to familiarize yourself with new vocabulary, you should also take the time to understand difficult concepts and passages. When you've had that experience of reading a paragraph or two, or perhaps even a page or more, without processing what it is that you've read, it could be that you've only read the words and haven't taken the time to see the relationship among the words, their meaning in the sentence. Whether you've zoned out for a period of time or just haven't understood what the author was trying to convey, you need to go back and reread and reassess those ideas.

In Chapter One, we mentioned that ardent active learners don't wait for class to begin the search for answers. The texts you'll read in college offer clues that can direct you toward such answers, and some of the most helpful clues are called references and end notes. Often considered ancillary material and, consequently, often unread, these resources are included by authors for a reason. They say, in effect, "Here is where you might look for additional information on the subject." References include information regarding a source of information. In this textbook, we've offered parenthetical references to the sources of information used. For example, journals allow "students and teachers [to] work together through written language to understand disciplinary content—its problems and its possibilities, and its value, usefulness, and connections to other disciplines and other situations" (Gardner & Fulwiler, 1999, p. vi). If you were interested in finding out more about journals, you would look for the full citation in the references section. There you would find all of the information you'd need to acquire the source from the library.

End notes differ from references in that they offer more than source information. End notes, typically found at the end of a chapter or article but before the references section, also offer some additional written commentary regarding a particular idea. This information was deemed to be interesting, though not crucial, for readers, and so was included in an unobtrusive way for the intellectually curious. References and end notes, then, can help you begin your search for answers—and these sources will have their own references and end notes to help keep your search going, if need be.

We don't always read for the same reasons. A student reads *Sports Illustrated* in order to get the latest information about a favorite player or team, and such information might be used in a conversation with friends or coworkers, though it might

Student Portrait

Ernie: "The summer of my junior year in school I remember I went to the University of Pennsylvania. I was talking to an admission person and they told me what kinds of grades I needed to get into school, and I was really discouraged and felt I would never get into a decent school. I think it's my reading that affects my grades. I've always been a really slow reader. Sometimes I read and don't remember what I read. And so now I kinda changed my ways a little bit, but definitely, since I got here, I've gotten a lot better."

just as well be used only for entertainment. This same student would have a different purpose when reading the "help wanted" section of the *Boston Globe,* a chemistry textbook, a stock report, or a short story for a literature class. Your method of reading should fit your purpose. Are you reading to get the main idea? Are you looking for important details? Are you trying to answer a specific question? Are you evaluating what you are reading? Will you be expected to apply the concepts about which you are reading? Recreational reading and academic reading require different levels of attention from readers.

You may be interested in learning to read more quickly. We've mentioned that there are times when reading quickly isn't ideal, but there are situations in which an increased rate is appropriate. Learning to read at an increased rate takes practice; you'll need to push yourself to read words more quickly, to skip unnecessary words, to focus on the more important sections, and to look for key ideas.

You might want to practice reading at an increased rate with your favorite magazine or newspaper. This material should be fairly digestible, and your familiarity with the format and layout will make it easier for you to navigate efficiently through the reading. You can also, of course, practice with other reading material. When reading a novel, for instance, try reading an entire chapter at an increased rate.

At times, you'll need to skim a text for a general impression. You might, for example, need to decide whether a book is relevant to the research you have undertaken. The title and/or subtitle has likely led you to this source; now you need to review the table of contents and index to determine whether the relevant topics are discussed, and to what extent.

Text Annotation Encourages Active Reading

Another way you can actively engage with what you are learning in college is to utilize text annotation, sometimes called marginalia. **Annotating text** means writing analytical, critical, and/or summative notes in response to a written work. This activity involves writing comments, notes, and questions in the margins, essentially establishing a written conversation between reader and text. Text annotation is a great way to stay on task and monitor your comprehension.

Why bother annotating text? For one thing, good readers react to what they read. We want to scream at the narrator in Ellison's "Battle Royal." How can he fall for the electrified rug trick? Doesn't he know that he's being used as entertainment? Why doesn't he refuse to fight Tatlock?

We feel for Matt Fowler in Dubus' "Killings." After all, is it that unthinkable that a father would consider avenging his son's murder as Fowler did? Who hasn't watched a news story about an abducted child and thought about what he or she would do if that were his or her child? When we think of our own child in this case, we are integrating the information into our schema. Literature forges connections between the fictional characters and the experiences of readers. Indeed, meaning is made as readers view the sequence of words on the page, filling in the blanks, and making pictures in their minds that represent the characters' actions.

Text annotation is a good way for you to react to literary works "within," "around," and "on" the work itself. The act of writing a comment or question may help you think through a complex idea. If you think of text annotation as an exploratory exercise, as an interaction with the text or a way to situate yourself around or within it, then this activity produces much more than just "notes."

Text annotation can be a great prelude to class discussion. When the professor asks students what they think about a character's actions or an author's thesis, the student who has annotated the text is not only likely to have a response, but is also able to quickly identify the section of the text that prompted the response.

Another reason to consider text annotation is, if you're anything like the rest of us, you don't memorize everything that you read. Text annotation provides a method of recording important elements of a literary work. In addition to reacting to a text, an annotation of "Killings" might very well include a note regarding the place(s) that Matt Fowler seemed to regret his vengeful actions. Such notes enable students to return to the text at a later date and more easily discover useful examples in preparation for an exam or writing a paper.

"Does anyone have questions about the reading?"

Text annotation also can be much more helpful than highlighting. Let's face it. Once you've highlighted a chapter in a novel or textbook, all of the highlighted information appears equally important. There is nothing to distinguish the significance of certain highlighted information from other highlighted information. In fact, when you look back at that chapter a week or two later, you often don't remember why you highlighted what you did! So then what happens? Yes, you've got to reread the highlighted portions, and probably the unhighlighted sections around them, in order to figure out what you were thinking during your initial reading. *Put down your highlighter.* With a pen in hand, you can identify important elements of a text while having the ability to identify why you've singled out that word, sentence, or "chunk."

The following is a list of suggestions regarding what an annotation might involve:

1. identifying a major theme of the work
2. questioning the morality of a character's thoughts and/or actions
3. identifying the central action of the work
4. noting the organizational pattern(s) exhibited in the work
5. identifying the author's intended purpose
6. making connections across works
7. examining differences across works
8. identifying with a character
9. asking a question you can't yet answer
10. stating the significance of a particular action
11. noting an event that you think is important
12. identifying a statement that doesn't seem to fit

Exhibit 4.2 is a sample annotated text. This sample annotation of Plato's *Apology* was done by a first-year student, Ashley. Notice how she was able to describe significant passages and concepts, facilitating future references. She also

EXHIBIT 4.2 | *Sample annotated text*

Impicty charge—

ASHLEY FABRIZIO

religious beliefs — Gods get power & give it to the wise. If you chip it away you chip away at the ideology — no purpose of Gods

APOLOGY

defence ↑

Socrates speech

What trial? ←

The Apology[1] professes to be a record of the actual speech that Socrates delivered in his own defence at the <u>trial</u>. This makes the question of its historicity more acute than in the dialogues in which the conversations themselves are mostly fictional and the question of historicity is concerned only with how far the theories that Socrates is represented as expressing were those of the historical Socrates. Here, however, we are dealing with a speech that Socrates made as a matter of <u>history</u>. How far is Plato's account accurate? We should always remember that the ancients did not expect historical accuracy in the way we do. On the other hands, Plato makes it clear that he was present at the trial (34a, 38b). Moreover, if, as is generally believed, the Apology was written not long after the event, many Athenians would remember the actual speech, and it would be a poor way to vindicate the <u>Master, which is the</u> obvious intent, to put a completely different speech into his mouth. Some liberties could no doubt be allowed, but the main arguments and the general tone of the defence must surely be faithful to the original. The beauty of language and style is certainly Plato's but the serene spiritual and moral beauty of character belongs to Socrates. It is a powerful combination.

literary — Plato artistic — Socrates

historical accuracy

Who is he? →

Courts similar to ours →

<u>Athenian juries</u> were very large, in this case 501, and they combined the duties of jury and judge as we know them by both convicting and sentencing. Obviously, it would have been virtually impossible for so large a body to discuss various penalties and decide on one. The problem was resolved rather neatly, however, by having <u>the prosecutor</u>, after conviction, <u>assess the penalty he thought appropriate</u>, followed by a <u>counter-assessment by the defendant</u>. The jury would then decide between the two. This procedure generally made for moderation on both side. > *Choose penalty*

Thus the Apology is in <u>three parts</u>. The first and major part is the main <u>speech</u> (17a – 35a), followed by the <u>counter-assessment</u> (35a – 38c), and finally, <u>last words</u> to the jury (38c – 42a), both to those who voted for the death sentence, and those who voted for acquittal.

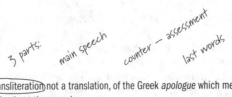

3 parts: main speech   counter – assessment   last words

---

1. The word *apology* is a transliteration not a translation, of the Greek *apologue* which means defence. There is certainly nothing apologetic about the speech.   *to jury*

continued

EXHIBIT 4.2 *Continued.*

audience/jury

I do not know, men of *Athens* how my accusers affected you, as for me, I was almost carried away in spite of myself, so persuasively did they speak. And yet, hardly anything of what they said is true. Of the many lies they told, one in particular surprised me, namely that you should be careful not to be deceived by an accomplished speaker like me. That they were not ashamed to be immediately proved wrong by the facts, when I show myself not to be an accomplished speaker at all, that I thought was most shameless on their part — unless indeed they call an accomplished speaker the man who speaks the truth. If they mean that, I would agree that I am an orator, but not after their manner, for indeed, as I say, practically nothing they said was true. From me you will hear the whole truth, though not, by Zeus, gentlemen, expressed in embroidered and stylized phrases like theirs, but things spoken at random and expressed in the first words that come to mind, for I *put my trust in the justice of what I say*, and let *none of* you *expect anything else*. It would not be fitting at my age, as it might be for a young man, to toy with words when I appear before you. → means bus

who is they

S P E A K E R

his words-truth

One thing I do ask and beg of you, gentlemen: if you hear me making my defence in the *same* kind of *language as* I am accustomed to use in the market place *by the bankers' tables*,[2] where many of you have heard me, and elsewhere, do not be surprised or create a disturbance on that account. The position is this: this is my *first appearance* in a lawcourt, at the *age of seventy*; I am therefore simply a stranger to the manner of speaking here. Just as if I were really a stranger, you would certainly excuse me if I spoke in that dialect and manner in which I had been brought up, so too my present request seems a just one, for you to pay no attention to my manner of speech — be it better or worse — but to concentrate your attention on whether what I say is just or not, for the *excellence of a judge lies in this, as that of a speaker lies in telling the truth* even though it must not sand right, it is true.

may be confusing to jury

defending himself 1st

It is right for me, gentlemen, to defend myself first against the first *lying accusations* made against me and my first accusers, and then against the *later accusations* and the later accusers. There have been many who have accused me to you for many years now, and none of their accusations are true. These I fear much more than I fear Anytus and his friends, though they too are formidable. These earlier ones, however, are more so, gentlemen; they got hold of most of you from childhood, persuaded you and accused me quite falsely, saying that there is a man called Socrates, a wise man, a student of all things in the sky and below the earth, who makes the worse argument the stronger. Those who spread that rumour, gentlemen, are my dangerous accusers, for their hearers believe that those who study these things do not even believe in the gods. Moreover, these accusers are numerous, and have been at it a *long time*; also, they spoke to you at an age when you would most readily believe them, some of you being children and adolescents, and they won their case by default, as there was no defence. Soc has been accused for most of his life.

has been accused for years

he has been accused from childhood experiences who is Anytus?

if they do not believe in god, then why do they believe the accusers?

→ no morales

2. The bankers or money-changers had their counters in the market place. It seems that this was a favourite place for gossip.

Used with permission of Ashley Fabrizio.

wrote questions at the point in the text where she had them, allowing her to have something to say in class when her professor asks, "Does anyone have questions about the reading?"

This chapter presented you with a variety of college-level study strategies. You were challenged to think about how you learn, practice using these strategies in different contexts, and develop a sense of when they would—and wouldn't—be effective. This first-year student accepted the challenge and has begun to develop her text annotation skills. Ashley's positive attitude toward change enabled her to attempt a new study strategy. Her locus of control was primarily internal, allowing her to see that she was, in large part, responsible for how well she would do in each of her classes. You need to decide whether you will accept the challenge to change, in addition to which new study habits you will adopt.

DISCUSSION QUESTIONS

1. In one of the student portraits in this chapter, Melodie reveals that she feels her high school did not prepare her for the rigors of college-level work. How do you think your high school prepared you? She also describes being "at the top" in high school and now she feels she's "at the bottom" in college. It seems that different high schools prepare students to varying degrees of readiness for college. Why do you think this happens?

2. Describe Colleen's attitudes toward learning from Chapter One. What are her locus of control and attitude toward intelligence?

3. In Ernie's student portrait, he expresses doubts about his reading abilities. Do you like to read? How do you feel about your reading load at college? How does your experience compare with Ernie's?

4. Do you believe intelligence is a fixed commodity, that you are born with a certain IQ (an entity view), or do you believe you can increase your intelligence through hard work (an incremental view)? Justify your position.

5. Both Gardner and Goleman challenge the ways in which we think about intelligence in our culture. Of the two theorists, with whom do you agree more? Base your answer on your own experiences.

6. Describe a time when you were stuck in an "automatic-thinking" mode. How were you able to get "unstuck"? What did you learn from the experience?

7. This chapter discusses different learning styles: auditory, visual, tactile/kinesthetic, and mixed modality. Which of these styles best characterizes the way in which you learn best? How do you know?

8. Analyze the teaching styles of your professors. Which of the learning styles best coincides with the ways each one teaches?

9. What could text annotation add to your reading experience? Are there any negative consequences of text annotation? If so, do the benefits outweigh the costs?

10. Besides the attitudes outlined in this chapter, what other attitudes can get in the way of student learning? Do you currently possess any of those attitudes?

ACTIVITIES

4.1 Using a reading that has already been assigned, read the text and use text annotation. Write a paragraph or two about the experience, particularly if this is your first attempt at annotation. Did you find that you were actively involved in the reading, more so than if you had used a highlighter, say? What types of notes did you make? How did this activity help you process what you were reading?

4.2 Regardless of whether or not you currently keep a journal, construct a journal entry focused on the way(s) in which you currently read literature and textbooks. Describe your reading process to an imaginary student with no college reading experience. Which elements of the process are you most comfortable with and which would you like to change?

4.3 Compose a journal entry that reflects upon the entry composed in Activity 4.2. Was this your first journal entry? Was this type of writing different from composing an essay? How so? What did you learn through this process?

4.4 Interview a sophomore and ask the student to compare the ways in which he or she approaches studies in his or her second year as opposed to in the first year. What particular differences can the student identify? Does the student mention any of the study strategies you currently use?

4.5 Create a list of the attitudes you possess that might potentially interfere with your learning. Identify the root of these attitudes (e.g., self-efficacy, past experiences with teachers, family influence, peer pressure). Generate potential solutions to help you guard against these attitudes "creeping in" and interfering with your goals.

REFERENCES

Anderson, S. G., & Anderson, C. E. (1992). Study skills made easy. *School Counselor, 39* (5), 382–384.

Cone, A. L., & Owens, S. K. (1991). Academic and locus of control enhancement in a freshman study skills and college adjustment course. *Psychological Reports, 68,* 1211–1217.

Dweck, C. S., & Leggett, E. L. (1988). A social-cognitive approach to motivation and personality. *Psychological Review, 95* (2), 256–273.

Friedman, V. J., & Lipshitz, R. (1992). Teaching people to shift cognitive gears: Overcoming resistance on the road to model II. *Journal of Applied Behavioral Research, 28* (1), 118–136.

Gardner, H. (1983). *Frames of mind.* New York: Basic Books.

Gardner, S., & Fulwiler, T. (1999). *The journal book: For teachers in technical and professional programs.* Portsmouth, NH: Boynton/Cook.

Goleman, D. (1995). *Emotional intelligence.* New York: Bantam Books.

Guild, P. B., & Garger, S. (1986). *Marching to different drummers.* Alexandria, VA: Association for Supervision and Curriculum Development.

Hadwin, A. F., & Winne, P. H. (1996). Study strategies have meager support. *Journal of Higher Education, 67* (6), 692–715.

Jones, C. H., Slate, J. R., & Marini, I. (1995). Locus of control, social interdependence, academic preparation, age, study time, and the study skills of college students. *Research in the Schools, 2* (1), 55–62.

Jones, C. H., Slate, J. R., Marini, I., & DeWater, B. K. (1993). Academic skills and attitudes toward intelligence. *Journal of College Student Development, 34,* 422–424.

Lefcourt, H. M. (Ed.). (1982). *Locus of control: Current trends in theory and research* (2nd ed.). Hillsdale, NJ: Lawrence Erlbaum.

Rabinowitz, F. E. (1987). A life transition seminar for freshmen college students. *Journal of College Student Personnel, 28,* 282–283.

Reynolds, J., & Werner, S. C. (1994). An alternative paradigm for college reading and study skills courses. *Journal of Reading, 37* (4), 272–277.

Reynolds, N. (2000). *Portfolio keeping: A guide for students.* Boston: St. Martin's Press.

Thomas, J. W., Bol, L., & Warkentin, R. W. (1991). Antecedants of college students' study deficiencies: The relationship between course features and students' study activities. *Higher Education, 22* (3), 275–296.

Turner, G. Y. (1992). College students' self-awareness of study behaviors. *College Student Journal, 26* (1), 129–134.

White, W. F., & Kitchen, S. (1991). Teaching metacognitive awareness to entering college students with developmental lag. *College Student Journal, 25* (4), 521–523.

Wratcher, M. A. (1991). Freshman academic adjustment at a competitive university. *College Student Journal, 25* (2), 170–177.

Developing Communication Skills

A s a college student, you'll be asked to communicate in various forums, through various mediums, and for various purposes. You'll ask questions in class; write journal entries; talk with faculty during office hours; and may even be elected to student senate, where you'll do some debating and public speaking. You'll instant message and email group members about important projects. In this chapter, we focus on three of the ways you'll be asked to communicate most frequently your understanding of material and come to a better understanding of that material: written assignments, class participation, and in-class presentations.

WRITTEN PRODUCTS VS. THE WRITING PROCESS

W riting is a process—an action—as well as a product—an object. Although students and teachers alike often focus on the end result of writing, the finished product, there are numerous activities that lead to the creation of a refined, final version. The act of writing— scribbling notes on scrap paper, talking out ideas with a friend, typing a paragraph into a personal computer or getting it down on paper—is a complicated set of activities that writers often take for granted.

To improve the quality of finished written products you are able to produce, you need to make changes in the way in which you go about producing them. Just as we have suggested that you be open to employing new study skills, so too do we suggest that you be open to considering making changes to your writing process. To help you do so, this chapter encourages you to examine the way you currently compose text, helps you evaluate that process, and offers some context-dependent alternatives.

Writing, as is studying, is often considered a solitary activity. Many people believe that a writer comes up with an idea, writes it down eloquently, and delivers the finished piece to an appreciative audience. Many people, those with an entity

---

IN THIS CHAPTER

- What communication skills will prove most helpful in college?

- What is the relationship between the writing process and the written product?

- How can you use feedback from professors to improve your communication skills?

- Is participating in class discussion really important?

- What does it mean to write a research paper in college?

- What makes for an effective in-class presentation?

view of intelligence, also believe that a fortunate few are born with a talent for writing and that the rest of us struggle to *seem* as though we can write. The truth is that good writing usually involves some degree of collaboration and revision, and anyone willing to put in the effort can become a strong writer, a concept aligned with an incremental view of intelligence.

Fairly recently, those who specialize in the teaching of writing have begun to challenge the notion that there is one writing process that all successful writers utilize. Supporters of what is termed the "post-process movement" contend not only that different writers have different—and equally valid/useful—processes, but also that writers use countless processes depending on the audience, purpose, and context of the writing they need to do (e.g., Olson, 1999). Instead of writing in the same manner regardless of the situation or audience, writers need to be able to modify their writing processes to fit different situations and audiences. Learning to be a better writer, then, means becoming more critically aware of the ways in which you write—another metacognitive activity—and being open to change.

You can write more successfully if you recognize (1) that the writing process takes time, for it is often more cyclical than linear; and (2) that starting early means you can take more time with each activity. Writing well often involves going backward before moving forward. You may decide, for example, that you need to generate additional evidence, an extended explanation, or an additional point after you have written a rough draft. You may decide that the argument you've constructed lacks a logical structure, so you make an outline from your draft and rework your organizational strategy. Just because you've got a version of your paper doesn't mean you can't continue to brainstorm, outline, and scribble.

The writing process, then, is far from a fixed, static set of steps to follow. Writers don't consistently proceed through such a series of steps to arrive at a final, written product; they do, however, engage in certain activities at different times during the writing process. These activities include prewriting, organizing, drafting, and revising, each of which we describe in more detail in the following sections.

Prewrite to Generate Ideas

At different points in the process of writing, you'll need to generate ideas. You'll need to think about the point you wish to make, the reasoning you'll use to support that point, and the evidence you'll provide to support your reasoning. Where do these ideas come from? Well, you might have started thinking about your topic in the classroom, perhaps during class discussion or while listening to a lecture. You've also most likely been doing some reading about your topic. This reading might have initially been limited to your textbook or the novel you were assigned, but your reading might also have involved some library research.

Regardless, you should have some thoughts about the topic you have been assigned, or have chosen, to explore. This exploration can occur through a stage of writing often referred to as "prewriting," work that comes before writing. This label is a bit misleading, because this activity *is* writing, not a detached, disposable precursor to it, and it often occurs at different points throughout the writing process, not only at the beginning.

Prewriting refers to the action of recording ideas with an emphasis on getting ideas in a form that you can see or hear. Prewriting is more about *what* you might say than *how* you might say it. The recording of ideas during prewriting might involve one of several different techniques, including brainstorming, freewriting, clustering, and tape recording.

The key to **brainstorming** is to let ideas flow from your mind through your hand onto paper without making judgments as to how to say things perfectly, how to arrange the ideas, or whether or not you *really* want to include a particular idea. Brainstorming is about recording as much of what you are thinking as possible so that you can make these judgments later. This, then, should be an energizing and freeing experience, for you're simply listing ideas as they come to you, letting the writing generate more and more thought.

An activity very similar to brainstorming is **freewriting**, a kind of prewriting that includes the formulation of "sentences" and "paragraphs" instead of the list of ideas that would result from brainstorming. Here, too, you should not be concerned with how you'll say things. Even though you are creating what look like sentences and paragraphs, the purpose of doing so is to encourage the continual flow of ideas. You can write more freely than you would if you were also concerned with relaying those ideas in grammatically correct form within a well-structured paragraph.

Clustering, also referred to as branching, involves a more visual approach. Here, ideas are presented graphically as they relate to one another. Clustering might look something like Exhibit 5.1.

| **EXHIBIT 5.1** | *Clustering ideas on* The Simpsons. |

If you feel that you can talk out ideas better than you can write, why not take advantage of your verbal abilities? Instead of putting your ideas down in writing, try talking them into a tape or digital voice recorder. With this technique, you can prewrite while driving a car, lying on a couch, or eating breakfast. Once you've recorded your ideas, simply play back the recording and jot down those ideas that seem most fruitful.

Which of these activities should you engage in when you prewrite? The choice is yours. You may decide to freewrite or you may decide to tape-record. Make your decision after you've engaged in some experimentation; try the different approaches to determine which works best for you. And try them for different types of writing: for different courses, for different professors, for different genres.

Selecting which activity to engage in or what approach to take when you prewrite should be based on your learning style. In Chapter Four, you were encouraged to familiarize yourself with your learning style to determine how you best study. Similarly, you'll want to consider your learning style when determining what strategies will work best for you during the writing process. For instance, visual learners may like to brainstorm on a sheet of paper for ideas or prefer clustering as a prewriting activity, so they can "see" the big picture. Auditory processors may talk with a friend or professor in an effort to generate ideas. Finally, tactile/kinesthetic learners may come up with their best ideas while taking a walk or through the use of manipulatives.

As mentioned, you will be better prepared to make your decisions about how to approach writing after some experimentation. Along with experimentation, though, comes serious reflection upon the way in which you write. Thinking about the way you write is yet another metacognitive activity, just like thinking about how you learn best. Remember, the most sophisticated learners have that knowledge and control over their own thinking and learning.

Organize Your Ideas

Once you've thought about which ideas you wish to include, it's time to think about the order in which you wish to convey them. This preliminary structure is certainly subject to change as you draft and revise.

It is often helpful for students to create a **logic outline** at some point early on in the writing process. This logic outline is devoid of roman numerals but does help writers think about what they wish to accomplish and how they are going to go about achieving these goals. Such an outline includes a *thesis statement,* a sentence that reveals the purpose of the paper, as well as the points the writer will offer in support of that thesis, referred to from here on as *supporting points.*

A logic outline might start out looking something like this:

Thesis: The members of the Simpson family have serious problems relating to one another appropriately.

Supporting Point #1: Homer and Marge both neglect their children, particularly Maggie.

Supporting Point #2: It is common for Lisa and Bart to assault each other physically.

Supporting Point #3: The Simpsons don't have quality conversations at mealtime.

Supporting Point #4: Mr. Burns isn't at all fond of Homer.

Supporting Point #5: Maggie was once alone in the wilderness for hours.

Creating such an outline will help you to present your thoughts in a clear, efficient, and organized way. It will also help you to identify overlapping or irrelevant points. In the example, for instance, supporting point #4 is irrelevant, because Mr. Burns's feelings for Homer don't support the notion that the *family* has problems relating to one another. The example also includes two overlapping supporting points, #1 and #5, the latter a specific example of the former. Supporting point #5, then, could likely be used as a specific example within the section involving Homer and Marge's neglect of their children.

Draft Your Ideas

Many students attempt to begin the writing process at the **drafting** stage. They sit at a blank computer screen or in front of a blank sheet of paper and try to compose a focused, well-organized, cohesive, detailed, engaging, grammatically correct draft. They worry about getting the first sentence just right. Not surprisingly, this often results in frustration and limited productivity—commonly referred to as "writer's block."

Drafting, in fact, does not have to begin with the creation of a first sentence or even an introductory paragraph. Many writers save that task until the very end of the drafting process, reasoning that they can't introduce readers to what will come next when there isn't anything yet there to reference. Drafting can just as easily begin with a supporting point or a paragraph that focuses on a specific example.

If you've created a logic outline, you've got some sentences already: your thesis statement, which is usually found in the introductory paragraph, and your supporting points, each of which can become a topic sentence for a paragraph or the focus of an entire section of your paper. These supporting points should be connected to your thesis via transitional words. These are words that bring your readers from one idea to the next, explaining, in effect, the relationship among sentences and paragraphs.

Using the Simpsons example, you might imagine the following topic sentence based on supporting point #2 of the logic outline:

Supporting Point #2: It is common for Lisa and Bart to assault each other physically.

Topic Sentence: Not only is this problem-family headed by two neglectful parents, but it also has two pre-teens who physically assault one another regularly.

The italicized words provide transition from the previous supporting point—Homer and Marge as neglectful of their children—to the next supporting point—Lisa and Bart's physical assaults on each other. Note that this transition also ties back into the idea you are trying to convey in the thesis—that the Simpson family has problems.

Once you've built this framework, you can drop in evidence to support the claims you've made. In other words, which Simpsons episodes show Lisa and Bart fighting with each other? What were the circumstances? You'd need to provide sufficient examples to support your contention that these violent exchanges are "regular" occurrences. The rule here is not to expect your readers to take your word for things. Instead, provide supporting evidence, whether it's mentioning a figure from a corporation's financial statement, referring to a failed marketing experiment, or quoting Hamlet himself.

Revise Each Draft

Once you've written a draft of a paper, letter, or resume, you should look it over to see if it needs **revision**. You may make changes because a word, sentence, or paragraph in the writing interferes with the meaning(s) you are trying to convey to your audience. It is a good idea to look for grammatical and spelling errors when reviewing a piece of writing, but there are other things to look for as well. Of at least equal importance are unclear and/or underdeveloped ideas that could be interpreted by an audience in ways you don't intend.

Different disciplines and writing genres follow somewhat different writing conventions. Although you will be introduced to some of those differences, the writing that you do in college—and the feedback you receive regarding that writing—will help you understand discipline- and genre-specific writing conventions. Some suggestions for revising and editing your work are as follows:

1. *Read your paper out loud to yourself.* This will give you two senses through which to process what you have written. It is oftentimes easier to identify an awkwardly phrased sentence if you hear it spoken. You can also try reading your work out loud to someone else or having that person read your work out loud to you. If you don't have a partner with whom to do so, try reading your writing out loud in front of a mirror. Writing centers are great places to learn more about and practice these techniques; we'll talk more about writing centers later in this chapter.

2. *After you've written a draft, wait a while before you revise it.* This may mean putting the paper aside for a couple of hours or a couple of days. Taking a break is a way to bring a fresh perspective to the piece—as long as the breaks don't become a means of procrastinating.

3. *Do not rely on the spelling and grammar checkers of word processing programs.* Microsoft Word, for example, will let you know which words may be misspelled and will even offer a suggestion to correct the "error." One problem is that Word often identifies correctly spelled words as errors. Another is that the suggestions are often worse than the original; computer programs can't "read," so they do

their best to "guess" which word you meant. And if your spelling was off significantly, the suggestion will be inappropriate, if not comical. Quickly typing "psleing" instead of "spelling," for example, results in Word offering the word "pulsing" as an alternative. Furthermore, the software program wouldn't even notice the problem posed by the sentence, "She wanted to go to." The careful student could surely identify these errors, but, oftentimes, students in automatic-thinking mode passively accept the program's recommendations without even looking at the screen.

A better alternative is to think of the red and green "squiggles" that Word uses under text to mark such errors as a warning system. You might reread these words, sentences, and paragraphs more carefully to be sure you've conveyed what you meant to, and correctly. Remember, though, that there may well be other words, sentences, and paragraphs needing your attention that the software has not identified as problematic.

4. *Try answering the following questions; doing so will help you think critically about your draft:*

- Does your thesis clearly relay the purpose of your essay?
- Do your supporting points all support your thesis?
- Did you give some thought to the way you've ordered these ideas?
- Have you supported the claims you've made with specific, concrete evidence?
- Have you checked to make sure you haven't made the same grammatical mistakes you typically make?
- Did you read the essay to yourself from start to finish? (Try reading it out loud.)
- Did you solicit feedback from your professor, a peer, and/or a staff member at the writing center?
- Did you use simple and concise language, rather than impressive-sounding language?

5. *Pay attention to grammatical issues as well.* Perhaps the most typical grammatical errors are sentence-level errors, including run-on sentences, comma splices, and sentence fragments. Though a discussion of grammar is beyond the scope of this chapter, you should gain access to a writing handbook, such as *The Prentice Hall Reference Guide* by Muriel Harris, in which you will find an explanation of these errors along with suggestions for avoiding them. It is equally important that you familiarize yourself with the grammatical errors that you usually make—identified on graded papers that have been returned to you.

6. *Find and correct spelling mistakes.* If you have any question about how a word is spelled—signified by a hesitation in thought when writing or typing the word—all you need to do is look it up in a dictionary. Because of the simplicity of verifying word spellings, teachers of all disciplines frown on spelling mistakes.

These errors signify a less-than-discriminating (i.e., lazy) writer. You should make a list of words that you usually misspell and study them, so that you can avoid making the same mistakes.

USING FEEDBACK TO YOUR BEST ADVANTAGE

There are several ways you can receive **feedback** on your written work: on the graded paper itself, during faculty office hours, through peer review, and via a consultation at the writing center. Each is valuable, and these methods should be used in combination to be most beneficial.

Your Faculty Provides Feedback via Graded Papers

> ### Student Portrait
>
> **Melodie:** "When it comes to writing I feel intimidated because I don't know. Like I was saying to my friend, I can just see Professor X thinking, 'You know, Melodie sucks at writing.' Like I get the impression they're *so critical*."

> ### Make It Personal
>
> What do you do with the feedback you get on your papers, quizzes, and exams?

Professors typically spend a great deal of time responding to the writing their students produce. Depending on the length requirements of a particular assignment, it is not at all unusual for a professor to spend half an hour or longer reading and commenting on a single paper.

Usually, professors' responses include four components: intertextual markings, marginal comments, an end comment, and a grade. **Intertextual markings** include things such as an inserted comma, a crossed-out semicolon, a notation of "sp" above a word to identify a misspelling, or a phrase deleted for conciseness. These markings are placed within the text itself, that is, above, below, or covering your actual words. In fact, the reason you are often asked to double-space your assignments is to allow enough space between each line of text for these markings.

Marginal comments occur in the (typically) one-inch margins surrounding the text. Here you might find a question your professor has asked in response to what you've written. You might also find arrows to suggest a better organizational approach. And you might find some of the same types of comments as you would within intertextual markings, although these comments are usually a bit more global in scope, concerning at least sentence meaning and often the significance of entire paragraphs.

End comments are even more global in nature. Professors usually include an end comment at the end of the paper, indicating its major strengths and weaknesses. This comment is based on the intertextual markings and marginal comments and is, in fact, an attempt to summarize them. The purpose of this end comment is to help students understand what they should continue to do in future papers as well as what they should work on improving.

Typically, the end comment is situated next to the numerical or letter grade that the student has earned. Unfortunately, this proximity often results in the end comment going unread, because students are tempted to focus solely on the grade, no matter what the grade is. It is, of course, important to focus more on the written feedback, for that is what will help you improve your work and/or enjoy continued success.

Faculty may offer feedback relative to your graded work in other forms as well. Your professor might insert written commentary within an electronic version of your paper. He or she may also offer verbal commentary via an audiotape or other recording medium. Typing and speaking are faster than writing longhand, so professors sometimes use such alternative feedback methods in order to provide more detail regarding their observations.

Faculty Can Also Provide Feedback During Office Hours

Faculty members hold weekly **office hours**, scheduled times when they are in their offices so that students can meet with them to ask questions or discuss problem issues. Additionally, many faculty members respond to student emails during office hours. It is a good idea to use these opportunities to get feedback on your writing. Clearly, the most useful time to do so is before a paper is due. You can solicit advice from your professor at any point in the process of writing, such as when the paper is first assigned, when you are refining a thesis statement, when you are organizing ideas, or when you are drafting. Consider this person your primary resource when doing writing for that particular course.

Your Classmates May Provide Feedback During Peer Review

Professors are not the only resource for writing support. You will, for example, likely be asked to perform **peer review** in one or more of your classes. Peer review, also known as peer group workshop, acknowledges the collaborative nature of the composing process, the understanding that writers and readers work together to construct meaning from text. Peer group workshops allow authors the opportunity to see how readers will respond to their texts—and to make changes based on these responses. To benefit from these workshops, you must be willing to listen to others' advice, remembering that your classmates will offer you *suggestions*. It is up to you to decide whether or not to implement them.

Your professor will usually explain the goal(s) desired and methods to be used in a particular peer review session. To help you make the most out of these experiences, we offer here some general advice. There is no one right way for you to review another student's paper, but there are some things you should keep in mind. The first is to have respect for your fellow classmate's work. Even though honesty is important when responding to what the author has written, intimidating or embarrassing remarks won't convince the author that your suggestions have merit. Such remarks result in a defensive posture, a situation that prevents constructive changes from taking place. To ensure that your advice is taken the right way, try phrasing your comments in question form. Do *not*, under any circumstances, give the typical, useless response, "Looks good to me." Although such a comment seems polite and neighborly, it won't help the author at all when it comes time for the piece to be judged a second time.

Another thing to keep in mind is that your advice will be far more on target if you take the time to read the entire paper before commenting. Focus on larger issues before mentioning things such as missing commas and confusing phrasing.

If your professor hasn't provided you with a list of questions to answer regarding your classmate's writing, you might consider some or all of the following:

1. Is the piece focused on the assignment? How does it (or doesn't it) fulfill the guidelines? Can the author do anything to meet the criteria more successfully?
2. What is the structure of the paper? Work backward to create a logic outline from the draft you are reading. Are the supporting points all relevant? Are there any overlapping points?
3. "Gaps" are places where more explanation and/or examples are needed to give the reader a clear understanding of what the author is trying to convey. Are there any "gaps" in this particular writing?

Remember that whereas the author is present and available to answer questions during your reading of her or his paper, this will not be the case when the paper is collected to receive a grade. Make sure these questions are addressed.

The Writing Center Is Another Great Place to Get Feedback

Your campus **writing center** can help you make writing assignments more manageable. Upon being assigned an essay, a report, a research paper, or another type of writing, you may be tempted to put off getting started, telling yourself that you "work well under pressure."

> **Make It Personal**
>
> Do you plan your time appropriately to put the necessary work into writing a good paper?

Remember, this is the credo of the die-hard procrastinator. Just as with studying, procrastinators will put less time into writing their papers compared with nonprocrastinators. A successful paper requires a sufficient amount of time and effort. Ask yourself, "Have I planned my time appropriately to put the necessary work into writing a good paper?" Here is evidence that time management is linked to your writing process.

It is strongly suggested that you start your papers early, meaning you should start to think seriously about an assignment the very day you receive formal instructions from your professor, *not* the morning the paper is due. Professors don't haphazardly assign writing in their courses; they have reasons for giving you the low-down on your team project two months in advance. One reason, of course, is that they think it should take a student that long to produce a paper that adheres to the stipulated guidelines.

Once you receive your instructions, try breaking down the paper or project into a series of deadlines in your daily planner. Force yourself, for example, to have an informal outline in a week and a rough draft in two weeks. If you do so, you'll find that you have plenty of time to visit your professor during office hours and meet with members of your writing center's staff *and* have time to make necessary changes once you've received feedback. Too often students find themselves disappointed and frustrated because they realize too late that they haven't answered the question their professor asked *and* their paper is due in two hours. By giving yourself deadlines, you'll reduce your chances of being in this rather hopeless situation.

Ultimately, you will learn more about yourself as a writer if you leave yourself time to reflect upon what you are writing. You'll get more out of each writing assignment if your writing process includes getting feedback from someone on the writing center staff, and doing so requires planning ahead.

The goal of any writing center is to help students become better writers. What these facilities offer writers is an opportunity to have their work read before that work is assessed for a grade.

The goal of any writing center is to help students become better writers.

Note that writing centers don't offer only "struggling" writers this opportunity; these centers can benefit *all* writers. This is an important distinction, because many think of writing centers as remedial resources, as places where poor writers go to get extra help. The truth is that poor writers don't often seek others to read their work; that's part of the reason their writing is less than effective.

If you aren't required to use your writing center through your first-year writing program or individual faculty, you can use the center as you see fit. You might visit the center multiple times for a single assignment, or you might stop by when you are getting started to be sure that your ideas are focused. You can visit the center to get started on a paper, to get feedback on a draft, to develop confidence about your writing, to clarify Modern Language Association (MLA) citation format (which we discuss later), or to reword a sentence for clarity. You might come to the center to use one of its reference books, or you might come to the center to write. Writing centers are *for* writers.

Though writing centers function differently from institution to institution, those who work there generally help writers become more aware of their writing strengths and weaknesses through focusing on the ways in which they compose text. For this reason, you would be likely to overhear a discussion about process upon visiting a writing center, namely the process students go through to arrive at the notes, outline, brainstorming, plan, and/or draft they brought to the session. Staff members also like to talk with students about what they plan to do with their work once they leave. Another common component of a writing center session is the discovery of new strategies, new ways of approaching writing, better ways to "react" when writing is assigned. If a student claims, for example, that he has never needed to brainstorm, that ideas are always plentiful, but the writing center staff member sees that the student's paragraphs lack development, the staff member might suggest that he give brainstorming another try. Such a suggestion is typically offered in the context of specific assignment guidelines.

Your preparation for, and active participation during, a session at the writing center will help you get the most out of the experience. It is important to remember that you are in control of what will happen; following are some tips to help you get the most out of the time you spend:

1. *Be open to suggestions.* The members of the writing center staff are not the "writing police." Their goal is to help you become a better writer. This can only happen when you are willing to talk about your writing *and* to listen to suggestions about that same writing.

2. *Provide the necessary background.* Your instructor has certain expectations for the paper you are trying to write, and those expectations can often be clarified by reviewing the assignment sheet during a consultation. By bringing notes, plans, and drafts, the writing center staff can see the journey your writing has taken and suggest where you might go next.

3. *Be prepared to explain the assignment.* You can visit your writing center at any stage in the writing process—whether it be when you are deciding on a topic, organizing ideas, writing an introduction, or revising a draft. Wherever you happen to be, however, you need to make a serious attempt at understanding the assignment. Be prepared to answer questions about the assignment and about your writing.

4. *Let the staff know what kinds of feedback you've received from your professor.* Although the session will focus on the paper you're currently working on, it will be helpful to both the staff and yourself to review the comments your instructor has made on your past work. What has your instructor identified on these papers as needing improvement? You'll want to be sure that the paper you're currently working on does *not* repeat problems you've had in the past and that it *does* repeat the things you've done successfully.

5. *Be realistic about what can occur in a single session.* What would you like to understand once the session is over? What bridge are you having difficulty crossing? What problem would you like to solve in a half hour to an hour? Don't hesitate to relate your goals for the session to the staff members with whom you are working; they will appreciate that you are using the time wisely.

PARTICIPATING IN CLASS DISCUSSION

You will learn and demonstrate understanding (and misunderstanding!) verbally, as well as in writing. This will occur in various contexts, including a discussion with a classmate after class, a group meeting at the library, and an argument over a reading of "Young Goodman Brown" in your residence hall room. In addition, many college classes require or encourage student participation in class discussion. Examine the syllabus from each of your classes to determine how class participation is defined and what emphasis the professor has placed on this activity. Many students resist participation, choosing not to ask questions or contribute to an in-class conversation. Here we explore the rationale behind class discussion so that you can make a more informed decision regarding whether you will be a regular participant.

In 1970, Paulo Freire, educator and theorist, criticized what he termed the **"banking model of education."** Ira Shor (1992), a Freirian scholar, explains this model: "Banking educators treat students' minds as empty accounts into which they make deposits of information, through didactic lectures and from commercial texts" (p. 31). One of the problems with this banking model is that it fails to consider the idea that students are not "empty accounts," that they in fact bring with them ideas, perspectives, doubts, and aspirations. Thinking of students as being acted *upon,* and not *actors* in the sense that they can affect change, is a dangerous notion. Adrienne Rich (1977), in *Claiming an Education,* felt so strongly about the difference between students acting versus being acted upon that she characterized it as the difference between life and death. Instead of adhering to a banking model, Freire poses what he calls the "problem-posing approach":

> Problem-posing education affirms men as beings in the process of *becoming*—as unfinished, uncompleted beings in and with a likewise unfinished reality. . . . The banking method emphasizes permanence and becomes reactionary; problem-posing education—which accepts neither a "well-behaved" present nor a predetermined future—roots itself in the dynamic present and becomes revolutionary. . . . Whereas the banking method directly or indirectly reinforces men's fatalistic perception of their situation, the problem-posing method presents this very situation to them as a problem. (quoted in Shor, 1992, p. 35)

So what does all of this have to do with class participation? Well, Freire would support student participation in the construction of knowledge, an idea that fits in nicely with the theme of claiming an education. Freire would argue that the opportunity to ask questions, to challenge statements made by the professor and/or other students, is crucial to a democratic education. Opting not to participate should be a conscious choice, one made with the understanding that in-class contributions will add to one's own learning as well as that of classmates and faculty.

Of course, not all classes include a class participation component. In others, professors assign a grade based on participation. Some professors don't assign a class participation grade but welcome questions during class. As an active participant in your education, it is important that you be clear on the way class participation will function in each of your classes. Do you understand what your participation grade will be based on, for example? What constitutes a successful contribution? How frequently are you expected to participate? Have you discussed classroom rules for respecting the views and opinions of others? If you don't have answers to these questions—or if you have other such questions—you should seek answers.

> **Make It Personal**
>
> Have you anticipated the focus for your next class? What will your professor likely discuss?

Some students are anxious about speaking in class. Take Justin, for example. Justin decides during his first day of class in political science that he will forego the 10 percent of his grade for class participation. He doesn't feel comfortable talking about things he doesn't really understand, and he doesn't want to look like an idiot—or a teacher's pet—in front of his friends. This isn't a big deal, he thinks, because he can still get a 90 in the class, and an A− isn't bad at all. But what is wrong with Justin's logic? To begin with, to earn that A− without contributing to class discussion, he'll have to get a perfect score on each exam and paper in the course, an unlikely possibility. Another problem is that he is basing his decision on avoiding "discomfort." Anxiety can lead to avoidance; Justin should seek to confront his anxiety, not avoid it. As a marketing major, Justin is working toward a career in which he must ask and respond to questions. Indeed, it is difficult to think of a career in which communication isn't an integral component. What we've been talking about since Chapter One is that college students need to be open to change, an attitude that is typically accompanied by discomfort. In other words, Justin should be seeking to move out of his comfort zone.

For Justin and others like him, confidence will come with practice. This means, of course, that at least for these students, initial contributions to class discussion will be anxiety inducing. If you are among this population, try to reduce the stress of these situations by coming up with a question or two outside of class. Anticipate the focus for your next class: What will your professor likely discuss? What central ideas, concepts, and/or examples do you expect will be the center of discussion? Preparing in advance, even practicing the phrasing of your questions or observations, will help give you the confidence you need to raise your hand in class and participate in discussion. After all, being prepared is bound to put you in a better position than some of your classmates, giving you additional confidence. You may even want to observe students who participate in class discussions regularly and model after those who do so with confidence.

Once you've developed confidence, you'll be more willing and able to share comments and ask questions that come to you during class, things you haven't prepared in advance. If you don't participate in class, you are missing a terrific opportunity to process material by discussing it and talking through difficult concepts. This mode of learning and studying material is the favored one for auditory processors. In a sense, they are doing some "studying" while in class. At the same time, however, all students can benefit. As we have pointed out, the most sophisticated learners figure out ways to cross over all three learning modalities in their studies. Participating in class provides you with the opportunity to cross into the auditory processing mode.

WRITING THE RESEARCH PAPER

What is the point of a research paper? A research paper consists of your contribution to an ongoing conversation (remember the Burkean parlor?) about a particular topic or problem, in effect a demonstration of your intellectual curiosity. The best research papers involve true discovery; although it is typical to have a hypothesis at the start of the research process, don't ignore your findings. You may very well end up trying to prove something different from what you originally imagined.

The research papers you write will be discipline specific. What follows here, then, is not a discussion on how to write a history, a literature, a psychology, or an economics paper, but some guidelines that are applicable, for the most part, to research papers in general. These guidelines are on formulating a research question, finding sources, evaluating sources, selecting and organizing material from sources, using evidence effectively, conducting research ethically, and using MLA and American Psychological Association (APA) format.

Formulate a Research Question

Oftentimes professors will offer students a list of research topics from which to choose or will, in some way, assign guidelines regarding topic selection. When this happens, you should resist the urge to just grab a topic and run with it. Instead, make your selection in a more calculated way. Choose several that particularly appeal to you, that you are genuinely interested in learning more about. You can then perform an initial library and/or Web search to see what is available about each of the topics you've selected. Acquire a few of these sources and skim them. Learning more about each of the topics will help you make a more informed decision. You will also be discovering how easy or difficult it is to find information relating to that topic.

Once you've decided on one of the topics offered, you'll usually have to *narrow your focus*. If, say, you've decided on "television violence" as your topic, you might consider a focus such as, "Television violence causes children to behave violently." You would find after doing some research, however, that there are many different types of shows exhibiting violence and that these shows are viewed by individuals of widely differing ages. Depending on the length of your paper, you would need to decide whether to narrow your focus to a subset of violent shows and their effect on one particular age group. Although it would be easy to find plenty of information relating to the broader focus for, say, a three- to four-page paper, the paper would be doomed to fail, because it is impossible to cover the material sufficiently in such a limited space. That focus is beyond the scope of the assignment.

Should your professor not have given a list of possible research topics, you will need to formulate one on your own. To do so, you might wish to consider the topics of conversation in class. Perhaps you could complicate or extend a point discussed in this forum. You might also wish to familiarize yourself with the topics most often explored in the particular field you are studying. Once you generate a few possible topics, it would be wise to do some of the preliminary research mentioned previously as well as visit your professor during office hours to discuss the possibilities. It's always a good idea to make sure you're headed in the right direction before becoming too invested in a particular topic and/or focus.

Find Appropriate and Useful Sources

Once you have a focus/main idea in mind for your research paper, you'll need to conduct a more thorough *search for relevant information*. There are a couple of ways to find books and articles that relate to your focus. One is to visit the library. Reference librarians are always glad to help you find what you need. These individuals know the library they work in better than you know your own home—so use their expertise to your advantage. However, if you are familiar with the library and want to begin on your own, you can search using the library's computerized databases, such as Ebsco Academic or Lexis-Nexis. These databases include information about magazine and journal articles that could be useful for your paper. By typing in keywords, you can search through thousands of articles in seconds.

Many campus libraries offer workshops for students about how to access and search computerized databases.

Once you've found books and articles, use them to find others. If there is a references page at the end of a work—and there usually is—scan it for other relevant sources. Authors have done their own thorough searches for information, so use their work to cut down on yours.

The Internet is another place to find sources. Through keyword searches similar to those you would perform to access information via the library's databases, you have access to incredible amounts of data through the World Wide Web. This searching is done with "search engines" such as Infoseek, WebCrawler, and Yahoo! Hyperlinks within Web pages can lead you to additional sources, similar to looking through the bibliography at the back of a book. Just as you would assess a printed book or article to verify that it is a credible and reliable source, you must do the same for Internet materials. Look for the name of the author, the date of posting, the last time the material was updated, and the citation of supporting evidence within the document. Your research must support the points you'll make in your paper, and the secondary sources you find should have evidence that supports the authors' statements. Be critical of what you read.

Evaluate Your Sources

All sources are not created equal. Your evidence could be critiqued as dated, irrelevant, biased, inconsistent with other findings, or otherwise unreliable. To be sure that you don't leave yourself open to such critique, it is important to do the following:

1. Check the copyright date if "currentness" is important.
2. Be aware of bias within sources: Do the authors have a stake in the issue? Do they benefit from their findings? For example, was the study showing that secondhand cigarette smoke isn't all that harmful performed by the Laramie Cigarette Company?
3. Search for professional publications (e.g., *Journal of Economic Literature, Political Science Quarterly, Black American Literature Forum*), because they are usually perceived as more credible than nonprofessional publications such as widely circulating magazines (e.g., *Newsweek*).
4. Scan a book to determine its relevance. Be deliberate. Check the title, subtitle, major headings, indexed terms, and bibliography.
5. Scan an article to determine relevance. Again, check the title, subtitle, major headings, and bibliography. You might read the introduction and conclusion as well.
6. Read and take notes actively. Be sure that you don't use information out of context.

You aren't reading for pleasure when you are looking for evidence—you need to read efficiently and carefully. This means scanning a source to identify especially useful sections. Once you are aware of these sections, you can make a point to read them more than once so that you have as clear an understanding of them as possible.

As you are reading, take notes, similar to what you would do when annotating text. These notes can take several forms: underlined phrases, bracketed lists, writings in the margin of a photocopied article or book chapter, writings on Post-it® notes, or color coding based on an outline. These notes should be made as you read; think of it as having a conversation with the text—make comments, ask questions, agree or disagree, interrupt. These notes will help tremendously, especially if time passes between when you read these sources and when you write the paper.

Read with a clear sense of what you are looking for: answers to questions you've formulated based on the preliminary outline you've generated. You are looking for information that deals with the focus you've chosen—remember this when you are ready to take notes. Ask yourself, "Does this have to do with my focus?" or "Where could I use this information in my paper?"

This is by no means an exhaustive discussion of techniques, but it is hoped that these suggestions will provide you with the means to begin gathering evidence in support of the focus you've tentatively chosen. Remember to ask questions—of your professor, of librarians, of tutoring center and/or writing center staff. They are all valuable resources that can help you smooth out the path to a successful paper.

Select and Organize Potential Material from Your Sources

After gathering a few articles, assess their usefulness by analyzing the title, abstract, and the first couple of paragraphs; decide whether the article will offer you insight regarding the topic you've selected. Once you've gathered what seem to be appropriate sources, it's time to start taking notes. As mentioned earlier, this initially includes bracketing, underlining, or attaching Post-its to identify useful information within these sources. Jotting down notes in the margin will be extremely helpful when it comes time to organize this information. Notes such as "possibly good for intro," "the opposition makes a good point here," "possible supporting point," "important," or "?" will tell you more than highlighting alone when you revisit these articles.

Before you begin compiling your notes in a more organized and useful fashion, make a list of the sources you plan on using so that you will have the bibliographic information necessary to do the references section of the paper. Consider this list a work in progress, because it will most likely change as you reread the notes you've made; you will decide some are more relevant than others and that you will need to acquire additional sources to fill in some gaps.

Once you've read through your articles and have identified the useful information within each one, you need to decide on a method of organization. How will you arrange the information you've found? You may decide to use index cards. You may choose scissors and tape. Other choices include markers or crayons, word-processing software, a three-ring binder, or color-coded Post-it notes. It's important for you to find a system of organization that you're comfortable with; remember, this system is supposed to make the process easier, not more difficult.

Here, we explain in some detail one of the systems: the *index-card system*. This system basically involves putting each piece of useful information on its own three-by-five or four-by-six-inch index card. By doing so, you will be able to shuffle them based on the main ideas found on the individual cards. On each card, in addition to the information, indicate which source you've cited from as well as the page(s) on which you found the information. This will save you time later when you compile your references. When writing the information onto the cards, you can quote, paraphrase, or summarize. Each use of ideas will need to be documented in your research paper. When **quoting**—copying down exact words from a source—put quotation marks around the text on your note cards. This will remind you to do so in your paper. When **paraphrasing**—putting someone else's language into your own words—you still need to give credit to the original author for her or his idea. When **summarizing**—reducing a long passage into a sentence or two—you still must provide documentation.

After you've generated all of your "note cards," read through them one by one to determine what is on each of them. Identify somewhere on the card (such as the back) how and where you think you'll use the information it contains. Does it include general information that might appear in your introduction? A specific example that illustrates one of your supporting points? Statistics that would strengthen part of your argument? Concluding thoughts? For example, if you've identified a quote that you think you might use in the opening section of your essay, write "opening." If you are researching the effects of Barney the dinosaur on his young viewing audience, you might identify a certain quote dealing with how the television show instructs through repetition. You would then write next to it "repetition."

This brief review will help you organize your stack of index cards into smaller stacks and, incidentally, create a pseudo-outline of your argument if you haven't made one already. After you've finished labeling this information (and you will, most likely, want to alter these labels at one time or another, which is fine), it is usually helpful to make an informal or even a formal outline before sitting down to start writing a first draft. Such an outline might look something like this:

Thesis: The children's television show *Barney* should change its instructional approach.

Supporting Point #1: Teaching involves more than just getting children to repeat what they hear.

Supporting Point #2: The show doesn't adopt a multicultural perspective, alienating many ethnic groups.

Supporting Point #3: Gender biases are being perpetuated through the show's themes and lessons.

When you write a section of the paper, you can have the stack of cards related to that section next to you, allowing you to manage your evidence effectively. If you get stuck, as writers often do, you can read through the relevant stack of cards for inspiration.

Whatever method you choose, the process of organizing this information should cause you to think about the reasoning you'll be using in the research paper itself. In other words, the points that other authors have made should help you think about the points *you* want to make.

Utilize the Evidence You Have Collected to Your Best Advantage

Research papers set out to prove a point, or sometimes a number of points. These papers are, then, to some extent, persuasive in nature. It is up to the writer to be as convincing as possible, and this can be accomplished in part through the effective use of evidence.

Why include documented information?

Besides the fact that doing so is often a requirement of the assignment, using evidence, which supports your ideas, is helpful for at least two reasons. First, this evidence can lead you to think about your subject in a different way. Material that you read during the research process strongly influences which points you will make as well as the conclusion you will make. Second, if selected for its relevance and included in the essay in strategic locations for logical reasons, this material can strengthen the argument you are making.

What makes evidence relevant?

Another way to phrase this question might be, "How do I know what information to use?" Including evidence within a paper means being selective. Quoting or paraphrasing goes beyond showing that you've read the texts in question: use these devices to verify what it is you are trying to say. Provide specific examples, whether they be a word, sentence, or passage, to illustrate the more general point you are making. Decide whether the information in question adds significantly to what you are attempting to communicate; in other words, would including it simply be redundant or does the passage in question introduce a new angle that you can elaborate on further?

How should I incorporate borrowed material into an essay?

When incorporating borrowed material, be concise. Quote only as much of the text as is necessary to impress a point upon the reader. Resist the urge to fill up your paper with borrowed material; this paper-lengthening tactic is obvious to instructors, and highly discouraged. Discuss or elaborate on every quote included. Remember that in citing material, you have taken it out of its original context. This means that you have had the benefit of reading the words, sentences, or passage in relation to the rest of the essay, story, novel, or other type of work, whereas the reader of your paper probably has not. For this reason, it is helpful to "introduce" quotes to the reader, sometimes identifying the person speaking in the quote, sometimes hinting at its content or relevance. After including the quote, it is necessary to discuss how it adds to what you have been (or will be) saying. Never let the quote speak *for* you, because it might say something you don't want it to say.

Following is a brief example of how to introduce, cite, and elaborate on a quote:

> *. . . Women are portrayed as housewives and sex objects in television advertisements. One television critic argues, "Women are portrayed exclusively as floor scrubbers, Band-Aid appliers, dish washers, and stain removers when they aren't strewn on a beach half-naked or drying off after a shower" (Smith, 1998, p. 25). These portrayals of women limit how they are viewed by society as a whole, mainly as dutiful housewives, nurturing mothers, and enticing sex partners. These ads ignore the large number of women who are in charge of multi-million-dollar companies or are professors at prestigious universities. . . .*

Student Portrait

Joe: "Quotes are great—are you kidding? If I have to get, like, four pages or something, double-spaced, a few long quotes really help. Know what I mean?
I usually try to use about four quotes, about one in each paragraph."

Conduct Your Research Ethically

As mentioned in Chapter One, it is important to give credit for others' ideas when writing. Whether quoting, paraphrasing, or summarizing a source, remember to use both in-text and bibliographic citations. Doing so will help you avoid **plagiarizing**, using someone else's words as if they were your own.

Academic writing often requires incorporating others' ideas. If these ideas are attributed to the appropriate sources, not only will you avoid plagiarism, but you will also demonstrate an ability to join a conversation in progress, as in the Burkean parlor, and make a contribution—in the way of summary, analysis, or synthesis, for example. To incorporate the ideas of others, you'll need to quote, paraphrase, or summarize. Quoting is appropriate when you'd like to use the exact phrasing found in the original source:

Student Portrait

Margaret: "I never know what I'm supposed to put in quotes. My English teacher used to tell us you don't have to use quotes if it's common knowledge.
I mean, most of this stuff makes sense to me when I read it, so why do I have to use quotes?"

Quoting Example

> *Richard Light's (2001) survey of more than 1,600 Harvard University students indicated that participation in extracurricular activities is quite common: "Seventy percent of all students are involved in two or more activities, and 14 percent are involved in four or five. Of those participating in any extracurricular activities, 68 percent invest more than six hours per week on average, and 34 percent spend more than twelve hours per week" (p. 28).*

Paraphrasing is used when you'd rather change the original phrasing, either for conciseness or to integrate the idea more clearly with what you said previously. When paraphrasing, be sure to indicate the source in an introductory phrase:

Paraphrasing Example

According to the results of Richard Light's (2001) survey of more than 1,600 Harvard University students, the vast majority of undergraduates participate in extracurricular activities, with some devoting more than twelve hours per week to these activities.

Note in this example that information was left out of the original quote, that choices were made regarding what was most important to reveal. This is similar to what happens when summarizing, the difference being a matter of scope. Whereas you might paraphrase a sentence or two, summarizing takes on larger portions of a text:

Summary Example

Richard Light's (2001) survey of more than 1,600 Harvard University students produced results indicating that there were definite factors influencing whether students had a positive undergraduate student experience. These factors include connections on campus, mentoring and advising, effective classes, engaging faculty, and campus diversity, among others.

Plagiarism, intentional or not, can have serious consequences. Lawsuits, failing grades, expulsion, and humiliation are all possible consequences of plagiarism. To avoid such disastrous consequences, consult with your professor or a member of your writing center's staff if you have any questions regarding whether to cite material.

Use Style Guides Effectively

MLA and APA citation formats have a reason for being. Investment bankers, psychologists, linguists, and other professional communities share systems of communication. These systems typically include, among other things, jargon that allows members to reference complex concepts quickly. They also include accepted rules for formatting particular types of documents; **MLA citation format** and **APA citation format** are two such sets of rules. These accepted standards allow members of particular professional communities to communicate more efficiently. These standards help to define the community: to identify easily who *is* a member of the community as well as who clearly *is not* a member. In other words, if you'd like your work to be taken seriously by your peers, you need to familiarize yourself with, as well as demonstrate a mastery of, the conventions of that particular scholarly community.

For your readers to be able to access the sources you've referenced, you'll need to provide some information. Both MLA and APA formats utilize a cross-referencing system, and the elements of that system are in-text citations and post-text citations. In-text citations occur when you reference the ideas of others within your own narrative. Whenever this occurs, it is important to let your readers know the source of the reference ideas. An in-text citation gives readers limited information: in MLA, the last name of the author (or authors) and page number of the reference are listed, and in APA the last name (or names) and the date of the source are listed. For a direct quotation in APA format, an in-text citation must also include a page number.

Another important element of this cross-referencing system is the post-text citation, a more detailed compilation of information regarding each particular source. If you reference a source in the body of your paper, you will also need to provide a post-text citation offering the details regarding that particular source in your references pages for APA format and in your works cited pages for MLA format.

A grammar handbook or an MLA or APA style guide offers a more thorough explanation of how to format in-text and post-text citations. These manuals are much broader in scope and include information on formatting, grammar, and other important topics. Equally important, these manuals include guidelines regarding citation format and offer examples for reference. The *Publication Manual of the American Psychological Association* is currently in its fifth edition, and the *MLA Handbook for Writers of Research Papers* is in its sixth edition. You can find these texts at your library or college bookstore.

MAKING IN-CLASS PRESENTATIONS

Much like an essay or research paper communicates your understanding of a particular topic or set of topics, an *in-class presentation* communicates what you have learned about a subject. You may be asked to do a presentation by yourself or with a group of students. These presentations may range in length from five minutes or less to an hour or more. You may be asked to summarize an essay, state a problem and pose solutions, present a business plan, or conduct other presentations that require you to do ample preparation beforehand and keep other things in mind during the presentation itself.

Professors typically offer guidance regarding these presentations, but there are some things you should know that will help you in such situations. When students prepare for an in-class presentation, they usually focus on the points they'd like to make and the evidence they will use to support those points, much as they would in an essay. Students also plan to have some type of overarching message, like they would for a thesis statement in an essay. Remember, however, that there are significant differences between communicating in writing and communicating in person.

Make It Personal
Do you think your audience will receive your message in the way you intended?

In addition to thinking about the logic of the presentation, you should consider the way in which the audience will perceive you, the speaker. When communicating in person, your audience will make judgments about your credibility, sincerity, and interest in the subject. If the goal of your presentation is to have the audience support your conclusions, then you will want to consider how you present yourself to them. If you don't seem to have considered the evidence fairly and objectively, if you don't truly seem to care about the subject you are speaking about, do you think your audience will receive your message in the way you intended?

There are ways to focus your audience's attention during the presentation and maintain a confident persona. As you may be aware, making eye contact with members of your audience will help you gauge the extent to which they are understanding what you have to say. You can also vary your vocal delivery. Try speaking more softly to emphasize a point—or more slowly. You might also try getting out from behind the podium or desk, in order to assume a more personal relationship with your audience.

In addition to using nonverbal communication, consider doing some audience analysis. Think about your audience as you prepare for your presentation. Why would your audience be interested in the topic(s) you'll discuss? How can you make your presentation particularly relevant for them? If you can engage your audience, your professor is likely to take notice.

If at all possible, elect to use talking points as opposed to a script. Reading out loud—whether from $8^1/_2$-by-11-inch sheets of paper or from PowerPoint slides—will make it more difficult for you to engage your audience, make eye contact, and demonstrate your mastery of the subject matter. Your delivery would be greatly improved if, instead, you prepare talking points, that is, notes to remind you about the points you want to mention. Of course, you'll need to be familiar enough with the material that you'd be able to speak effectively about the topic from memory. Having such familiarity will require ample practice.

You'll likely be asked to do some *group presentations* in college. Since there will be multiple speakers during these presentations, there are additional preparatory activities. First, at least one of the group members should look through the notes for each speaker. The goal in doing so is to identify any contradictions and unplanned redundancy. Second, the group should consider how to make the entire presentation flow. For instance, the second speaker could summarize the first speaker's comments and mention how the upcoming information relates to earlier comments. This transition between speakers could be something like: "As Sarah explained, it is important to identify possible training issues early on. I'll now discuss other potential problems with introducing a new software package, including compatibility issues and stability." Transitional statements and phrases help your audience make the connections you want them to make, increasing the likelihood that they'll see how your supporting points and evidence support your overall message.

Finally, don't perform the presentation for the first time in front of the class and your professor. Recently, a group of four students gave a presentation on tutoring. The group was overly confident and didn't perform a run-through of the presentation prior to the actual event. This proved disastrous. They began with their first point—but hadn't remembered to introduce the members of the group or the title of the presentation to the audience. Ten minutes into the presentation, they recognized their error and took time out to do belated introductions, making their presentation fragmented and disjointed. The lesson here is to practice your presentation as many times as necessary beforehand to work out any problems and to ensure that things will go smoothly when it is time for your work to be assessed. It would probably be helpful if you could have an individual not affiliated with the group or class to give constructive feedback. Chances are, if that individual has trouble understanding how a piece of evidence is relevant or needs clarification regarding a particular statement, your classmates—and professor—could very well respond the same way.

Here is a summary of important points for making in-class presentations:

- Make eye contact with your audience.
- Vary vocal delivery.
- Vary physical proximity.
- Utilize visual aids.
- Prepare talking points instead of reading.
- Provide transitions between speakers in a group presentation.
- Practice your presentation, in front of an audience if possible.

The previous chapter asked you to think about your study habits and strategies and how you might change them to meet the academic demands of college. Similarly, this chapter challenged you to reflect on your communication skills and how you will need to work on honing them to meet the heightened expectations of your professors. With that in mind, we have provided you with a variety of sound suggestions to respond to the various forums where you will need to demonstrate your communication skills. One important question remains: Will you heed the advice offered in this chapter? That is, will you change the way in which you use feedback and how you approach writing papers, and will you make a concerted effort to participate in class discussions? You have control over your answer—either you can change or you can remain situated in the familiar.

DISCUSSION QUESTIONS

1. In one of the student portraits in this chapter, Melodie talks about feeling intimidated by her professor's response to her writing. How do you imagine professors will respond to your writing? How have you handled feedback in the past?

2. What types of patterns have you observed in the way that professors respond to your writing? What types of comments typically emerge?

3. What do you do with the graded papers professors return to you? Do you ever react emotionally? Why or why not? How does using feedback relate to active learning? If you wanted to discuss a writing assignment with your professor, what would you bring to the meeting during his or her office hours?

4. Do you always use the same process regardless of what you are writing? If not, how does your process differ depending on the writing task? How do the stages in writing processes presented in this chapter compare with those you use?

5. How do you go about finding useful information for research papers and projects? How do you take notes for a research paper? How do you organize the information you find? What is plagiarism? How do you know what is common knowledge and what needs to be cited?

6. What is the purpose of research? What do research papers have in common with other types of writing you have been asked to compose? What makes research papers different from other types of writing?

7. Describe what happens during peer review. Is this a useful exercise? Why or why not?

8. When should you visit the campus writing center? What should you expect to happen during this session?

9. How could you work backward from the due date of a paper in your daily planner? How could you slice up the work into manageable chunks?

10. In this chapter, Justin decides to avoid class participation because he isn't comfortable talking in class. What aspects of college make you uncomfortable? What would it take for you to move out of your comfort zone? What differentiates you from students like Justin? What do you have in common with him?

ACTIVITIES

5.1 Practice criticizing your own writing. This activity involves creating a "metatext" for a piece of writing you've composed recently. Using a paper you have already submitted for another course, create an accompanying document that explains how you went about composing the original piece. Describe your writing process for this particular paper by answering the following questions as specifically as possible:

- How did you arrive at your focus/thesis?
- Did you have an organizational plan? (If so, how did you decide on this plan?)
- Did you draft the paper in a single sitting or in multiple sittings?
- Where did you work on this paper? (You can include more than one setting.)
- Did you solicit any feedback while working on this paper? (If so, from whom? How did you use the feedback?)
- How happy were you with the outcome?

5.2 Seek feedback regarding a piece of writing on which you are currently working. You may visit your professor during office hours or meet with someone at the writing center. After you've done so, record your thoughts regarding the experience. Was the meeting productive? Did a second set of eyes help you see things you couldn't on your own? How could the meeting have been improved? What did you learn about yourself as a writer?

5.3 Logic outlines are a great way to ensure that your writing stays focused and organized. Create a logic outline for a paper you have not yet drafted *or* create a logic outline from the draft of a paper on which you are currently working.

5.4 Compose a journal entry in the form of a letter to an incoming student at your college or university. Offer this individual insight into what she or he should expect when writing a college paper. What have you learned so far about professors' expectations? What tips could you give this student?

5.5 Take a trip to the library. Conduct an initial library search to see what is available about one of the topics you will be researching for another course. If you haven't yet been assigned a research paper or project, simply choose a topic you are interested in learning more about. Search a database such as ProQuest to find sources related to your topic. Don't hesitate to ask the reference librarian for help if you need it. Print out a list of four or five relevant sources, including one journal article.

5.6 When searching the Web for information, users certainly hope that what they find will be reliable and useful. Write about the ways you verify the reliability and usefulness of a website. Here are some questions that will help deepen your response:

- Can the reliability of information found via the World Wide Web be determined?
- What about the nature of Web pages might make them less reliable than, say, an article in a scholarly journal?
- Should users be more critical of websites than of more traditional publications?
- What distinguishes a reliable website from an unreliable site?
- Are commercial sites a better source of information than private sites?
- Are so-called official websites somehow more valid than "nonofficial" sites? Why or why not?

5.7 When you have a draft of a paper you are working on, try reading your work out loud to yourself—as if you were giving a speech. What did you notice about your writing as a result of this exercise? Does this seem like a useful technique that you might repeat in the future? Why or why not? How might you modify this technique to reveal more about your writing?

REFERENCES

Light, R. (2001). *Making the most out of college: Students speak their minds.* Cambridge, MA: Harvard University Press.

Olson, G. (1999). Toward a post-process composition: Abandoning the rhetoric of assertion. In T. Kent (Ed.), *Post-process theory: Beyond the writing-process paradigm* (pp. 7–15). Carbondale: Southern Illinois University Press.

Rich, A. (1977). Claiming an education. Speech delivered to the students of Douglas College, Rutgers University, New Brunswick, New Jersey.

Shor, I. (1992). *Empowering education: Critical teaching for social change.* Chicago: University of Chicago Press.

CHAPTER SIX

Combining Readings and Notes for Optimal Performance in Lectures and on Exams

You will face many points in the semester when your professors will expect you to demonstrate mastery of course material. That is, they will expect you to show them what you have learned. Some of the places where you will showcase your knowledge are on quizzes, tests, and exams. Facing the testing situation in college is inevitable; thus, this chapter covers the major facets of testing: test preparation, test taking, and self-evaluation.

Unlike in high school, you can no longer afford to think of test preparation as what you do the night before a test. In college, test preparation includes all of the activities you accomplished before sitting for the test, basically all of the study strategies you applied starting from the very first day of the semester. To do well on your tests in college, you have to think about how you prepare for tests as well as how you take tests. Essentially, you must employ your metacognitive skills: thinking about how you tend to learn material for your tests and questioning how your methods impact your test performance.

You'll need to ask yourself a variety of questions: Did I do all of my assigned readings? Did I fully understand everything I read? If I had questions regarding the reading, did I seek out answers on my own? Did I visit my professors during their office hours? Did I take adequate notes in lectures? Did I design and take practice tests to be sure I understood the material? Did I seek out learning assistance, such as requesting a peer tutor to help me when a term or idea was unclear? The list of questions goes on and on. The point to all of these questions is for you to **self-evaluate**, for you to be completely sure that you did everything within your power to prepare adequately for the test. Evaluating your test preparation strategies gives you valuable feedback. If you can honestly say that you adequately prepared for a test, and you still are not successful, you will know that your area of weakness in testing is not with test *preparation*, but may be with test *taking*.

> **IN THIS CHAPTER**
>
> - What are the best ways to take notes in college?
>
> - How can you best reconcile class notes with out-of-class notes on the reading?
>
> - Why are study groups a popular study strategy?
>
> - How can you be sure you are prepared for an exam?
>
> - What can you do to improve your performance on true/false, multiple-choice, short-answer, and essay questions?

Phil: "I studied for the material. I thought I had the material down enough before the test. I got the test, read through it and realized I didn't understand the stuff enough to take the test. I got nervous and brought the test up to the professor and said I couldn't take it."

Make It Personal

What habits and personality traits do you possess that may be preventing you from applying the strategies you have learned?

Student Portrait

Rupa: "I can't believe I didn't start studying until the night before. I stayed up until five in the morning and didn't even hear my alarm clock. Why do I always have to pull all-nighters before every test?"

After this chapter helps you to evaluate your test preparation strategies, it covers general approaches for taking multiple-choice, true/false, and essay tests. Having a general approach to tackle these types of exams will help reduce your anxiety when you are in a test-taking situation. Having a plan of action always helps; however, what is often more powerful is learning from past mistakes.

The best way to determine whether your testing weaknesses come from the test preparation situation or the test-taking situation is to diagnose your errors on a test or an exam on which you have received feedback. Look at the items marked incorrect. Can you find each of these items in your text or notes? Answering this question is crucial. If you cannot find the correct answers, your notes are probably incomplete. You would then know that note taking is a skill you need to develop. When it comes to questions on a test that were derived from readings, you will have to determine why you may have missed the important information and analyze your reading skills in relationship to the strategies outlined in that text.

Perhaps the most powerful information that self-evaluation and diagnosis of errors on your tests will give you is a "reality check" as to whether you are actually using the study strategies you have been taught. At this point in the semester, you have likely learned at least a few new study strategies and know what you should be doing; the real question is, are you actually doing these things? If not, you may need to reflect on your motivation and attitudes again: what habits and personality traits do you possess that may be preventing you from applying the strategies you have learned?

THE COMPONENTS OF TEST PREPARATION

As mentioned, test preparation begins on the very first day of class. What you do on a daily basis ultimately affects how you will perform on an exam. Study skills specialists and psychologists have observed and researched what the best college students do regularly that allows them to perform to the best of their ability. Consistent patterns have emerged among the top students in various schools and among students of widely divergent backgrounds and abilities. Although many students succeed in academic settings, certain techniques stand out that any student, no matter how well prepared in high school, can apply. The following techniques—considering how course objectives might be used on tests, taking notes, connecting ideas, gathering feedback, asking questions, implementing prereading, and studying with a group—used by savvy students, are all activities that contribute to adequate **test preparation** (White, Mikulecky, Lake, & Ginn, 1986).

Be Aware of Course Objectives

Successful students focus their attention on the *course objectives*. This may seem obvious, but it appears that the average student has the attitude, "If it's in the course, I have to memorize it." Most professors introduce too much information to allow for memorization. Also, most professors are not impressed with simple memorization of details. They want to know whether you can apply, compare, and employ the concepts and thinking strategies presented in the course. How can you find out what the course objectives are? Professors usually relay this information in the course syllabus, at the beginning and end of classes or lectures, and in directions for assignments. What you will want to do is consider how the course objectives might be used on a test or an exam. For example, if one of the goals of your Earth Science course Human Impact on Land and Life is to develop a thorough understanding of the issues involved in the misuse of land and wildlife management, you can expect to see an essay exam item that might read something like this: "Describe four key issues that are involved in the misuse of land in the Brazilian rain forest."

Take Comprehensive Notes

This brings us to the second characteristic of highly prepared students: they take **comprehensive notes** in classes and lectures. Comprehensive means complete notes with all levels of information, including generalizations, examples, explanations, transitions, questions, introductions, summaries, and repetitions. Students will say, "But my teacher told me to just write down the important things." The professors can say that—they already know what the important things are, and they are so familiar with their fields that they are able to remember details. Students, however, can't always tell what is important, and they will likely forget a significant portion of the lecture if they don't write down enough information. So, as one study skills specialist advises, "Write as much as you can down, and figure it out later. You can't write down everything!" Many students find that by going into a lecture with the objective of writing down everything, and by writing continuously during the lecture, they can record almost everything they need. Two additional advantages of writing everything down are that it forces you to use your kinesthetic learning modality, and it keeps you listening actively throughout the whole lecture. We address note taking more extensively later in this chapter.

Connect Important Ideas

Another skill successful students possess is the ability to *make connections* between the "whole" and the "parts." That is, they can usually identify what the most important ideas, concepts, or relationships are in a reading, laboratory, lecture, class, or work of art, *and* they figure out how each part is related to the main points. For example, if the notion of "self-concept" is presented in a lecture, these students will watch and listen for examples of self-concept in readings and class discussions. Good students figure out what's important and anticipate what will be expected. An effective strategy for figuring out what's important is synthesizing notes and readings, that is, taking your class notes and checking their accuracy against the information in your text. Doing this will allow you to determine whether you've missed any important points.

Gather Internal Feedback

Make It Personal

How do you know when you've figured out what's *really* important?

How do you know when you've figured out what's *really* important? That's another strategy of good students: they establish **feedback procedures** to determine whether they understand the subject. The most common sources of feedback are study groups, professors, upperclassmen who took the course, and writing center or other learning assistance staff. Students can gather internal feedback by using some of the following strategies: predicting questions that might appear on exams; making summary sheets; tutoring other students; and self-testing, in other words, covering up notes or closing a textbook and *saying* everything aloud (for auditory learners) or writing down everything that can be remembered (for kinesthetic learners).

Ask Questions

Perhaps the single most significant characteristic of the best students, and the way in which they prepare for exams, is that *they ask a lot of questions*. These questions fall into two categories. First, in reading and listening, these students silently ask questions of the author or lecturer. Put another way, they form hypotheses and then read or listen to see if they have predicted correctly what will be said next. This is where text annotation comes in again. For kinesthetic learners, writing down the questions in the margins of their books will help them remember the information more readily.

Perhaps the single most significant characteristic of the best students, and the way in which they prepare for exams, is that they ask a lot of questions.

Second, questions can also be asked of other people: in classes, tutorials, conferences with professors, and meetings with learning specialists. Remember, this is a learning style strength favored by auditory processors. Auditory learners benefit greatly from questioning professors, other students, upperclassmen, staff, and tutors. All successful students, though, find out where they can get help when they need it. They get to know their professors, counselors, and professional staff by talking with them. They find out where they can get help for study skills, reading, math, and course material. They find out who could be of assistance with personal, academic, and administrative problems. They find out who the best students are, which upperclassmen have had the same course or professor, and which tutors can help them.

Successful college study strategies may seem to be common sense, but all of the strategies call for action on your part, and applying the strategies begins on the first day of classes, not the night before the first test.

To Read Actively, Preread and Record Pertinent Information

We discussed active reading and text annotation in Chapter Four, but one additional way to prepare for tests is by engaging in prereading strategies. These activities will help you better understand what you are reading—the first time through—as well as help you generate organized and efficient notes from the reading.

By this point in the semester, you've probably realized that you are expected to do *lots* of reading in college. You're probably expected to read several chapters (or more!) every night. Despite the volume of reading, your goal shouldn't be to see how quickly you can tear through a chapter. We have already addressed how reading passively often results in simply staring at words that have ceased to have meaning—reading "in the zone," so to speak, where your eyes are seeing, but your brain isn't processing.

You'll be a more effective and more efficient reader if you engage in some preliminary activities before your "word-by-word" reading begins. The prereading activities that follow are designed to help you become a better reader of college textbooks. Although performing these tasks will, admittedly, take some time, you will find that doing so means you will have a fuller understanding of what you read.

The first of these preliminary, or prereading, strategies is to look at the title of the chapter. Besides recording this information in your notebook as the beginning of an outline, you should use the title to predict what you will be reading. Are you familiar with any of the words or phrases used in the title? What do you already know about these concepts? This reflection will give you a foundation on which to build an understanding of new information.

In addition to considering what you already know about the topics suggested by the chapter title, you should consider how this chapter fits among other chapters in the text as well as other material presented in class or referenced on the course syllabus. Here you are concerned with understanding how the chapter you are about to read relates to the totality of material you will be reading for the course.

Another useful prereading strategy is to skim the introduction to the chapter, listing key points, sequencing ideas, and perhaps even writing your own brief summary paragraph. Doing so will help prepare you for what is to come and is a particularly effective exercise for kinesthetic learners.

Before you read the chapter in earnest, you should consider creating an outline. By this point, you've already recorded the chapter title. Now add the first main heading; subheadings; and, under each subheading, the content vocabulary words (i.e., those words that are emphasized in bold or italics). Be sure to record page numbers next to each item so that you can easily access the information in the textbook as necessary. Exhibit 6.1 is an example of a chapter outline that employs this method.

| **EXHIBIT 6.1** | *Sample chapter outline.* |

I. Sleep and Dreams (Myers, 1999, p. 173)
   A. Biological rhythms and sleep (circadian rhythm) p. 173
   B. The stages of sleep p. 174
      1. R.E.M. sleep
      2. Alpha waves
      3. Hallucinations
      4. Delta waves
   C. Do we need sleep? pp. 176–77
      1. The effects of sleep loss
      2. Sleep theories
      3. Sleep disorders pp. 178–79
         a. Insomnia
         b. Narcolepsy
         c. Sleep apnea
         d. Night terrors

Finally, after creating a chapter outline, this outline can be used for additional studying. You might try, for example, putting the outline into paragraph form. You could also study the outline and then self-check your understanding of the material by seeing how many questions you can answer at the end of the chapter.

Study with a Group

Although we have focused in this chapter, for the most part, on what you can do to study on your own, there is no need to study in isolation. In fact, many students create study groups for this purpose, and these study groups can be quite beneficial. Simply discussing course material with others—as opposed to memorizing—is a great way to learn new concepts and practice applying new analytical methods. Study groups also have the benefit of multiple students' perspectives on classroom lectures, discussion, and text readings. Each member can have a more comprehensive set of notes through the efforts of the group. In other words, if you were unable to transcribe the professor's example in class, chances are one of your group members has the example recorded.

Of course, groups don't just originate instantly and begin to work at the height of productivity. It is inevitable when groups of people live, work, and study together that they will progress through certain developmental stages. According to Bruce Tuckman (1965), a theorist interested in how groups evolve, these stages are forming, storming, norming, performing, and adjourning. **Forming** involves a group getting together to work toward a collective goal and determining members' strengths and weaknesses. Here the group discusses how to approach the task at hand. **Storming** occurs when conflict arises, an inevitable occurrence. The group must resolve these conflicts before proceeding to the next stage, norming. **Norming** is when the group agrees on guiding principles or rules that each group member must abide by for the group to function most productively. The **performing** stage is when the group performs effectively and productively— that is, if it reaches this stage. **Adjourning** involves establishing closure for the particular project involved.

When you are assigned a group paper or project, or even when you are assigned to work in a group in a classroom setting, your group will naturally progress through some or all of these stages. The roles of each individual member will affect the group's ability to progress through these stages.

To consider how you might function as a group member in college, it might be helpful to think about the first group of which you were a member, your family. Oftentimes the role that you play in your family will emerge when you participate in other groups. If, for example, you were the mediator of disputes in your family, settling arguments among siblings or between siblings and parents, you might be inclined to want to resolve disputes in your marketing group. If you were the oldest member of your family and took responsibility for taking care of your younger siblings, you might be compelled to "take care of" your group members. You might, for example, feel the urge to follow up to make sure that your group members completed their tasks. To use a popular culture analogy, the characters on the television show *Friends* fulfill specific roles in their group. Chandler is the group clown, always telling jokes to relieve tension. Ross is the responsible, levelheaded one. Monica is the obsessive caretaker. Do you know what role you occupy within your family and your primary group of friends? How might this role affect your participation in a group project or study group?

The stages of group development can tend to be a long, laborious process. The college semester is only 15 weeks long, so if you decide to join a study group or you are assigned a group project, you don't have the luxury of allowing your group to proceed naturally through these stages.

For the group to be as productive as possible, group members should consider setting some rules and procedures. These could include information about meeting length, frequency, and location. The group might also decide that food, drink, and music aren't conducive to a serious, businesslike study situation (White et al., 1986).

Your group should agree on a structure for meetings (White et al., 1986). You might decide, for example, that each meeting will be a review of the readings and lectures for the week. Everyone in the group, then, would have to complete the readings and review notes before each meeting, so that the meetings can focus on identifying and mastering key concepts. The study group might also decide to collectively draw up a summary sheet for the course, listing main topics and important subtopics. Each of these topics and subtopics would then be discussed so that everyone can have a thorough understanding of them.

APPROACHES TO NOTE TAKING

Jean doesn't take notes in her astronomy class. Writing down what the professor is saying and writing on the board seems like a waste of time, because the professor seems to spend most of her time illustrating key concepts using examples that aren't in the textbook. Sometimes she even defines these concepts differently from the textbook. The textbook offers definitions for each key term along with an example, so Jean relies solely on the book for her notes. Besides, this approach means that she can relax and take everything in during class.

The true test of Jean's approach to note taking will come with the first astronomy exam. Jean is making some rather flawed assumptions:

1. that the textbook's definitions supersede those of the professor
2. that the examples offered in the textbook are sufficient toward illustrating each concept
3. that the examples offered in class are similar to those offered in the textbook (i.e., redundant)
4. that the exam will be based on the textbook and not class notes

Other potential problems with this approach to (not) taking notes is that Jean will likely be less engaged in the class and more likely to daydream, do other work, or not attend class. Participating in class discussion will be more difficult for such disengaged students. Finally, Jean's professor is likely to notice this behavior, depending on the size of the class, and attribute it to laziness, disinterest, or even disrespect.

Have an Organized System of Taking Notes

Students should have a system of note taking and a notebook that keeps their notes organized. Many students find that using a three-ring binder with several pockets for notes and other materials is the most efficient way to be organized (Lister, 1993). Using a three-ring binder is efficient, because it allows you to keep notes and handouts in order. If you get a handout that goes with a particular lecture, you can punch it with three holes and keep it in your notebook alongside the lecture notes. This method also enables you to record your reading notes or study group notes on loose-leaf paper, so that you can place that information with your lecture notes as well. Keeping all relevant material together will make life easier when it comes time to study for tests.

Good note taking requires being attentive and employing active-listening skills during lectures. Students should develop a personal system of note taking that works for them. Judicious use of a highlighter to make certain information stand out in notes is useful. Just as the author of a textbook highlights important information in bold print, you can use a highlighter to mark information that you deem important in your own notes, making it easier to locate that information. There are several other things you can do to take better notes:

- Some time during the semester, you will begin to get accustomed to your professors' various lecture styles. At this point, try to listen for signal words in a lecture, rather than try to write everything down. Signal words will provide directional clues to alert you to important information. Listen for clues such as, "The two areas are . . . " or "In conclusion . . . ". Whenever a professor raises a question in a lecture, write it down and listen for the answer. You can almost guarantee that this question will appear on an exam (Longman & Atkinson, 1991).
- Don't necessarily copy notes over to make them neat. Instead, write neatly from the start. This is another strategy to keep you on task with your listening comprehension during lecture. If you begin to write sloppily, you are likely losing concentration (Lister, 1993).
- Don't erase mistakes but, rather, draw a single line through the error. This will prevent you from losing your thoughts during the lecture (Lister, 1993).

In addition to these note-taking techniques, you should develop your own abbreviations for taking notes, your own shorthand, which we discuss next.

Use Shorthand When Taking Notes

Taking notes in class requires you to be able to record information quickly and accurately. Because it is impossible for most of us to transcribe a lecture verbatim with no errors, you need a system to make note taking more manageable.

One such system is to formulate a key that allows you to abbreviate major concepts and commonly used words and phrases. These concepts and commonly used words and phrases will change, to some extent, from class to class, and it may take some time to develop the key.

Sharon Alex (1999), a study skills specialist at Becker College in Massachusetts, offers a sample key for an Introduction to Chemistry course (see Exhibit 6.2). Notes written using this sample key might look something like those shown in Exhibit 6.3.

You'll want to keep your key handy—this method won't be very effective if you forget how to translate your own shorthand. Try translating the following statement using the keys offered in Exhibit 6.2:

b/c he dn't → t * directions b/f going to class t student was ∴ unable to cont t class.

In addition to developing a more efficient system of taking notes in class, you should consider using a note-taking system that allows you to synthesize your class notes with notes you've generated from course readings. One system designed for this purpose is the Cornell system of note taking.

EXHIBIT 6.2	*Sample Key.*

MAJOR CONCEPTS KEY		
Enz = Enzyme	P = Products	Mol = Molecule
Sub = Substrate	R = Reactants	Engy = Energy

COMMON WORDS KEY					
b/c	= because	w/	= with	2'	= two
+	= and	t	= the	$\longrightarrow$	= follow
*	= important	c	= with	rt	= right
$\therefore$	= therefore	b/f	= before	dn't	= didn't
w/o	= without	2	= to	cont	= continue
intro	= introduction	a/f	= after	lf	= left

Used with permission of the author.

Coordinate Your Class/Lecture Notes with Your Reading Notes

The **Cornell system of note taking** allows students to coordinate their lecture notes with their reading notes. This approach to note taking involves following

EXHIBIT 6.3	*Example of notes using key in Exhibit 6.2.*

Enz Function

Sub are R in chemical reaction
Enz 1. Lower temp
     2. Engy ↓
     3. pH
Sub + Enz → P + Enz

Specificity—Active site

certain procedures. To begin, you can try one of two things: you can either write down your notes only on the right side of your notebook and leave the left side for a work sheet (or vice versa if you are left-handed) or divide the paper on which you are taking notes into two columns. In each case, implement the Cornell system, the components of which consist of the five Rs: Record, Reduce, Recite, Reflect, and Review:

Record: Take your notes during a lecture on the side of the page you have designated for that purpose.

Reduce: Either in the left margin or on the left side of your notebook, summarize your notes as soon as possible after the lecture.

Recite: Cover the column where you took your notes in class. Using the summary in your "reduce" column, see if you can recall the information.

Reflect: Think about the material discussed during the lecture. Try to formulate a question that may be asked on a quiz, a test, or an exam. Record the question in the "reduce" column, a question that your notes in the "record" column answer.

Review: Review your notes regularly. You may actively review your notes by comparing them to what the text says about the same topic or concept. You may want to write down the text material in your notes, but in a different color, so that you can easily distinguish the source of information. Jot down the page number for a quick reference; this will save time when you study.

Exhibit 6.4 is an example of a page of student notes using the Cornell system of note taking. Note the way this page of chemistry notes is broken up into sections, with possible exam questions listed in the left margin, and the notation of page references.

THE BENEFITS OF EMPLOYING THE VARIOUS APPROACHES TO STUDYING

Now that you've been exposed to a variety of study strategies to prepare you for exams, the question is, will you use them? It is time, once again, to reflect on your attitudes toward learning and studying. There are many advantages to taking a systematic approach and implementing all of the strategies you've learned. These strategies:

> **Make It Personal**
>
> Now that you've learned various study strategies to prepare you for exams, will you use them?

1. *Encourage the use of all three learning modalities.* Outlining a chapter will create a visual representation of the concepts and allow you to see the part-to-whole relationships in the text, a visual processing activity. Active listening and questioning in lectures will tap into your auditory processing mode. Taking comprehensive notes is your kinesthetic activity.

2. *Help you create schema to guide reading comprehension.* Outlining a chapter and recording key terms will help you create a mind map of the information. This will

EXHIBIT 6.4	*Student sample of Cornell system of note taking.*

REDUCE	RECORD

State the differences between protons, electrons, and neutrons (p. 24)	I. Atoms: The Stuff of Life (pg. 24)
	   A. Protons—positive charged subatomic
	     • weight 1 amu (atomic mass unit)
	     • found in nucleus
	    Electrons—negative charge
	     • no weight
	     • found in energy levels (orbits)
	    Neutrons—no charge
	     • weight 1 amu
	     • found in nucleus
	     • it stabilizes nucleus

Information added from text

What is atomic mass? How is it found? (pg. 25)	number of protons determines atomic number of an atom Atomic mass=sum of protons and neutrons (pg. 25)

Information added from text

What is electricity?	Electricity—Flow of electrons (pg. 24–25)
	   Opposites—attract
	   Likes—repel
	     H ⊙ 1e ——HYDROGEN (H)
	   B. Isotopes (pg. 25)
	     • atoms with a different number of neutrons
	Some elements exist as mixtures of different isotopes
	Deuterium—hydrogen atom with 1 neutron ——→
	[Hydrogen atoms do not have neutrons]
	Tritium—hydrogen atom with 2 neutrons ——→
	Energy levels (pg. 29); 1st—2 3rd—18
	           2nd—8 4th—32

What is the rule of Octet?	Rule of Octet—most atoms like 8 electrons in outer energy level This makes the atom Happy :O)

Information added from text

	Chapter 2
What is PH?	PH (pg. 37) • hydrogen ion concentration Hydrogen w/out electron is an ion The more you have the more acidic it gets
What is a hydroxyl?	OH—hydroxyl—oxygen & hydrogen W/extra electron base or alkeline PH scale (pg. 37) Anything below 7 acid [lower the # stronger it gets] anything 7—neutral; above 7—base Acid released hydrogen ion or proton
What is a base?	Base—something that takes on protons Ex. Bio cd (7.35 PH)

Explain a buffer.	Buffers (pg. 38)
	   • help to maintain PH
	   • take H ions out to make acid
	Co in H2O make carbonic acid Most of the time naturally produced

What are the waves from?	Alpha—weakest; Beta—stronger
Weakest to strongest?	Gamma—starting to get dangerous; X-ray—can be very dangerous

enable you to check your vocabulary and begin to familiarize yourself with difficult terms and concepts. Once you see the big picture with your outline, you'll be better able to learn the supporting examples and details that relate to the new concepts.

3. *Increase listening comprehension for lectures.* The exercise of outlining a chapter prepares you to listen well in lectures. When the professor mentions a new concept in a lecture, your familiarity with the concept and its relationship to other concepts will facilitate greater understanding.

4. *Allow you to generate a list of all key terms and concepts.* Many times students will say, "I have no idea what's going to be on the test." Using the outlining strategy produces a list of all the concepts in the chapter you'll need to know.

5. *Discourage memorization (unlike flash cards) and let you tap into higher-order thinking skills.* Memorization is a lower-order thinking skill. Higher-order thinking skills are application, analysis, synthesis, and evaluation.

6. *Help you to predict test questions.* Taking the headings and subheadings in your text and turning them into questions may give you some insight into what will be asked on a test. While you are at it, design some multiple-choice questions using those words in bold print.

7. *Assist you in time management practices.* For example, if you outline on Monday, go to class and take notes using the Cornell method on Tuesday, synthesize your notes and your readings on Wednesday, and review material with your study group on Thursday, you are breaking your study time up over a few days (spaced practice) instead of cramming (mass practice).

APPROACHES TO TEST TAKING

E very test is unique; therefore, there are limits to the advice offered in the remainder of this chapter. The following sections are designed to give you insight into three of the more common types of test questions: multiple choice, true/false, and essay question/prompt.

Advice for Taking Multiple-Choice Exams

Savvy students find out what a test or exam format is beforehand, because they recognize that the format will influence how they study for the test. If a test is multiple choice, some students will gear up for tough study sessions, because they know from past experience that this test format is an area of weakness for them. Some students, on the other hand, will breathe a sigh of relief when they hear that a test will be multiple choice. They think, "Phew, I won't have to study as much now. All of the answers are right there, and all I have to do is choose the right one. I'll have a one-in-four chance of picking the right one." Such students lull themselves into complacency when it comes time for multiple-choice tests.

Most multiple-choice tests tend to be derived from readings (textbooks in particular) as opposed to class notes, which means good reading comprehension is the key to success on these tests. For those who have procrastinated, avoided their readings, or haven't bothered to try some of the college-level study skills presented in this book, multiple-choice tests in college will likely present a problem. To do well on a multiple-choice test, knowing the structure of your textbook and corresponding notes is a must. Look again at the outlining strategy introduced in this chapter (see Exhibit 6.5). Now focus on a particular section of the outline. Doesn't "C3" look like a multiple-choice item? Using this outline strategy helps you identify the possible source of test questions. "Sleep disorders" is part of the potential stem of the item, and "a," "b," "c," and "d" are among the potential answers. Insomnia, narcolepsy, sleep apnea, and night terrors were the concepts that appeared in bold print in your chapter.

EXHIBIT 6.5   *Sample chapter outline with note.*

I. Sleep and Dreams (Myers, 1999, p. 173)
   A. Biological rhythms and sleep (circadian rhythm) p. 173
   B. The stages of sleep p. 174
      1. R.E.M. sleep
      2. Alpha waves
      3. Hallucinations
      4. Delta waves
   C. Do we need sleep? pp. 176–77
      1. The effects of sleep loss
      2. Sleep theories
      3. Sleep disorders pp. 178–79
         a. Insomnia
         b. Narcolepsy
         c. Sleep apnea
         d. Night terrors

A potential multiple-choice question

Imagine that all you did was memorize these definitions, however. Say, for example, you made a flash card, with the word "insomnia" on one side and the definition "a sleep disorder involving recurring problems in falling or staying asleep" on the other. This strategy might have worked in high school, where you might have seen a multiple-choice item that tested you on recall of memorized information, perhaps looking something like this:

1. The following is a sleep disorder involving recurring problems in falling or staying asleep:
   A. insomnia
   B. narcolepsy

C. sleep apnea

D. night terrors

In college, however, you are likely to see a more complex item, one that tests your higher-order thinking skills such as application, synthesis, and analysis. The test item that follows, for instance, requires you to think about the concepts more deeply:

2. All of the following sleep disorders have the potential of threatening a person's physical safety except:

A. insomnia

B. narcolepsy

C. sleep apnea

D. night terrors

For this test item, you'll need to think critically about each possible answer. In class, it was mentioned that there was speculation that the captain of the ship involved in the *Exxon Valdez* oil spill was an insomniac, which caused extreme sleep deprivation. He might have fallen asleep while piloting the ship. This example (application) was discussed in class and did not appear in the text. You compared your notes and your readings as you studied (synthesis), so you know the danger insomnia poses.

From your text reading, you learned that narcolepsy is when a person has uncontrollable sleep attacks and lapses into REM (rapid eye movement) sleep at inopportune times. The text states,

> Those who suffer from narcolepsy—1 in 1,000 people estimates the National Commission on Sleep Disorders Research—must live with extra caution. As a traffic menace, "snoozing is second only to boozing" says the American Sleep Disorders Association, and those with narcolepsy are especially at risk. (Myers, 1999, p. 170)

Again, understanding examples is the thinking skill of application.

In your notes, you have recorded that sleep apnea is when people stop breathing while they are asleep. Sounds dangerous—that could certainly be a physical threat. However, in your reading of the text, you found this explanation regarding sleep apnea: "A sleep disorder characterized by temporary cessations in breathing during sleep and consequent momentary reawakenings" (Myers, 1999, p. 170). You also know that sleep apnea causes irritability the following day, and spouses of sufferers complain about the snoring common to this disorder, but nowhere in the text did it mention physical threats to the individual with sleep apnea. You need to analyze this.

Finally, you look at night terrors. Night terrors happen mostly to children. Unlike nightmares, they are characterized by high arousal and an appearance of being terrified. Sufferers may get out of bed and walk around even though they are still asleep. This poses a danger to small children afflicted with this disorder, who could fall down stairs or otherwise trip or fall and injure themselves. You now go back to the stem and reason that the only sleep disorder that is likely *not* a physical threat to the sufferer is sleep apnea. The process of reasoning through this college-level test item is quite a bit more complex than for the first sample item.

What if the multiple-choice item looked like the following sample? This item relies on recall but is complicated by the vocabulary found in the text:

3. A sleep disorder characterized by temporary cessations in breathing during sleep and consequent momentary reawakenings is:

   A. insomnia

   B. narcolepsy

   C. sleep apnea

   D. night terrors

You are back to relying on your notes. Your notes say that sleep apnea is when people stop breathing during sleep. Although question #2 is a recall question, you didn't read the text and aren't sure what "cessations" means. It sounds like it might mean "stops." You're a little nervous taking the test because you avoided the reading. Seeing the unfamiliar vocabulary word makes you feel even more panicked and contributes to your test anxiety. If only you had synthesized your text and notes, you would have seen the word "cessations" before and given yourself the chance to clarify its meaning. The bottom line: what separates the most successful students from the rest is that they are intimately familiar with their readings and notes. They have achieved close to 100 percent mastery of the material that has been presented to them whether it's from the lectures or readings. They also have a strategy for taking multiple-choice tests; what follows is one such strategy.

Refer to the multiple-choice item in Exhibit 6.6. Read the stem, "All of the following sleep disorders have the potential of threatening a person's physical safety except," and note any qualifying words, in this case, "except." Next, determine the

---

EXHIBIT 6.6   *Using key and qualifying words.*

3. All of the following (sleep disorders) have the potential of threatening a person's (physical safety) (except:)

   A. insomnia

   B. narcolepsy   key

                         concepts   qualifying

   C. sleep apnea   word

   D. night terrors

key concepts in the question, in this case, "sleep disorders" and "physical safety." Determine the exact context in the course. You recognize that this item has been derived from a chapter entitled "States of Consciousness" and appeared under the main heading "Sleep and Dreams." You have now established the part-to-whole relationships. If you know the answer, mentally answer in your own words before you get confused by the distracters, different phrasing, or vocabulary presented in the potential responses.

Check *every* answer. See if you can determine whether each answer is true or false. Insomnia has the potential of threatening a person's physical safety. True or false? If you get confused, go back to the stem and try to complete the item in your own words and then find the closest meaning. Be careful about distracting answers that may be from the same context, but are irrelevant. Also watch for those that are from similar concepts, or have qualifying words or prefixes. After the first test in a course, you can often see what kind of distracting answers are being used. If there is more than one answer, choose the one that is more true. After selecting an answer, always check the stem quickly to see that you haven't forgotten it or have ignored a qualifying word such as "except."

You might also try taking the "thrice" approach to going through your multiple-choice items. The first time through, read the stem and cover up the answers. If you've studied well, you should not have to "cheat" and look at the answers provided on the test. Attempt to come up with the answer in your own words before you look at the responses provided. Go through the test once using this strategy, and mark items you were unable to answer. The second time through, use the classic process of elimination strategy, eliminating those responses you know aren't correct and making an educated guess using those remaining. The third, or last, time through, on the items on which you can only hope to guess, resist choosing absolutes such as "all of the above" and "none of the above." Eliminate similar choices, and choose the longest, most detailed answer. Remember, use this last method *only* when you are forced to guess.

Advice for Responding to True/False Items

Many students get very nervous about true/false items on objective tests. Provided that your preparation is adequate—that you have utilized the suggested reading and study strategies outlined thus far—there is a way to approach true/false items. Read the item as if it were a rule that has no exceptions. For example:

T F   1. All of the tissue in the central nervous system is neural tissue.

Answering this item correctly requires you to understand two concepts: (1) that the brain and spinal cord make up the central nervous system and (2) that neural tissue is tissue consisting of neurons or nerve cells. Knowing this information depends on the level of your test preparation (what you did before the test) as opposed to test taking (what to do when taking the test, what you are learning about right now—tips for reading true/false items). Assuming that you are prepared, your job is to see if you can come up with an exception to the "rule":

All of the tissue in the central nervous system is neural tissue.

If you are unable to identify an exception, the item is true. If you can come up with an exception, the item is false. In this case, the item is false. You know this because some, albeit very little, of the tissue in the central nervous system is connective tissue. You identified an exception. Consider the same "rule" with just one word altered:

***Most** of the tissue in the central nervous system is neural tissue.*

With true/false items, changing one word can change the correct answer. In this case, constructing the item with the word "most," instead of "all," accounts for the exception(s). Awareness of this requires you to read each item carefully, noting any limiting words or phrases, just as you would with a multiple-choice item. A successful true/false item strategy, then, involves

- reading the true/false item as if it were a rule with no exceptions.
- checking your level of preparedness, making sure you understand the concepts (key words or phrases at the heart of the item) clearly.
- noting any limiting words or phrases such as "some," "many," "all," or "few."
- identifying any exceptions to the rule, accounting for the limiting words and/or phrases.
- answering based on the presence or absence of an exception: if you are unable to identify an exception, the item is true, if you can come up with an exception, the item is false.

In-Class Essay Exams Don't Have to Be Daunting

Professors often require students to compose an essay in response to one or more prompts on an exam. These essay responses constitute all or part of the exam, which might also include other types of questions, such as multiple-choice, identification, true/false, matching, or short-answer questions.

Essays written in this particular situation tend to invoke anxiety from a substantial number of students. It isn't difficult to imagine why this might be the case, in large part because this writing situation is different from that of a take-home writing assignment. Comfort level, space, immediacy, and available time are all limited during an in-class essay exam, more so than with a take-home writing assignment. You may very well feel less comfortable in these situations. This is partly owing to the fact that you aren't likely to know precisely which topic(s)/question(s) you'll be asked to respond to on the exam. You also aren't able to write in a space of your choosing. Whereas writers often have one or more conducive places where they do their work, composing an essay exam response usually means writing at a less-than-comfortable desk with pen and paper. There won't be the poster you look at to help you focus your thoughts or the computer with which you write more quickly. In fact, you may find yourself distracted by the classmates writing around you ("He's done already?!") or the sounds of maintenance workers outside your classroom window. This situation also means that you can't decide when you'd like to get started writing. You have a limited amount of time, and you need to begin the process as soon as possible. This process is often modified as a result of time constraints.

Because much of students' anxiety surrounding in-class essay exams is a result of such situational differences, it makes sense that these anxious feelings might be diminished if the situations weren't so different. What, then, can you do to make in-class essay writing more like take-home essay writing? For one thing, you can try to make yourself as comfortable as possible within the confines of a classroom environment where respect for the professor and fellow classmates is expected. A cup of coffee, favorite pen, or lucky sweatshirt might help these exams seem a bit less daunting. A seat toward the front of the room may limit the extent to which you are distracted by everyone else working on their own exams.

Another way you can make in-class essay writing more like take-home essay writing is to engage in some of the same writing activities. Although time is, admittedly, limited, much can be done with a little time management. Consider a 50-minute exam period, for example. If you normally do some brainstorming before creating an outline and draft, you might give yourself 5–10 minutes to brainstorm, 5 minutes to create a draft, and 25–30 minutes to compose a draft. If you write on every other line, you'll leave yourself room to go back and revise/edit—and you'll have 5–15 minutes remaining in which to do so.

Here are some additional suggestions for taking essay exams:

1. Make sure you understand the question or prompt; if you don't, get clarification.
2. Don't assume that structure, transition, and grammar don't count. These are all important because they allow your reader to understand the ideas you are attempting to convey in the manner in which you want them understood.
3. Don't try to tell your professor anything and everything that you know. Stay focused on answering the question or responding to the prompt.
4. Be specific when possible. Offer examples and illustrations that demonstrate a more thorough understanding on your part.
5. Be aware of how much time your professor has allocated to the essay. If you finish too early, it could be that your professor is looking for a more developed response than the one you've provided. Use the extra time to provide an additional supporting point and/or to illustrate existing points with detailed examples.
6. Write legibly. This is something you can check when you review your work. Your professor can't commend what she or he can't read.

SELF-EVALUATION OF PREPAREDNESS FOR QUIZZES, TESTS, AND EXAMS

Think you are ready for your next test, do you? The following questions, developed by Heidi Brown (1996), formerly a social science learning specialist at Boston University, are designed to allow you to self-assess how prepared you are for an upcoming quiz, test, or exam. If you can answer "yes" to most of these questions, you are probably well prepared. If you find yourself responding "no" to some of these questions, you may want to engage in some additional preparation and/or plan on doing things differently for the next such examination.

ARE YOU PREPARED?

INSTRUCTIONS: *Write Yes or No to respond to each question.*

_____ 1. Did you spend a portion of your study in a group of at least 3 people?

_____ 2. Did you study by units? Did you coordinate readings with lectures?

_____ 3. Did you write questions in the margins of your class and laboratory notes, questions that the notes were answers to?

_____ 4. If yes, did you use these questions to test yourself after having studied the notes?

_____ 5. Did you use the class and lab lecture outlines to test whether you could summarize the entire lecture in a few minutes (i.e., look at the outline and recite the major points of the lecture)?

_____ 6. Based on the class lectures and the readings of each unit, did you make a list of all the terms, concepts, and theories you should know?

_____ 7. Did you restate all definitions, concepts, etc. *in your own words* (orally or in writing)?

_____ 8. Did you work at linking authors and their ideas/theories and their concepts?

_____ 9. Did you use all of the study guides you may have received?

_____ 10. Did you review past tests, quizzes, etc. and determine your areas of weakness?

_____ 11. Did you discuss past "problem" quizzes, etc. with your professor in an individual meeting?

_____ 12. Did you *actively* read *all* of the assigned readings, restating main points in the margin in your own words, summarizing sections, making outlines, and relating them to lectures?

_____ 13. Did you use your texts and/or a dictionary when a term or idea was not clear?

Used with permission of Heidi Brown.

In many ways, this chapter asks you to think about all that you've learned from the *Foundations for Learning*. For instance, "Is the night before your first test in college the time to begin thinking about whether your high school–level study strategies will serve you in college?" In effect, you begin preparing for your tests and exams the minute you step into the classroom at the start of the semester. The testing situation will raise a variety of issues for students. The decisions you make regarding how you take notes, how you read your texts, and whether you join a study group will have a greater impact than drinking a pot of coffee to cram the night before an exam.

DISCUSSION QUESTIONS

1. What makes memorization a problematic study technique?
2. How do you approach multiple-choice test items? How efficient and effective is this approach?
3. What should you do if you earn a lower grade than you expected on a quiz, a test, or an exam?
4. Do you take notes in the same manner in each of your courses? What are your reasons for doing so or not doing so? How might your professor's instructional methods affect the notes you produce?
5. In this chapter, a system for synthesizing textbook and class notes, the Cornell system of note taking, was reviewed. What other system(s) could provide the same function? How do you currently combine class and textbook notes?
6. When you reach the point where you feel you are prepared to sit for a test or an exam, how do you know you are ready? What kinds of feedback techniques do you use?
7. What test format(s) do you prefer? Why do you think this is so?
8. Compare your preparation techniques for a test on which you performed well with your preparation techniques for a test on which you performed poorly. What were the key differences?

ACTIVITIES

6.1 Practice for an upcoming essay exam. Generate questions that you think may appear on the exam, and after studying, attempt to answer the questions in the time allotted for the actual exam. This exercise will help you see where you should focus your remaining studying.

6.2 After a test has been returned to you, see if you can diagnose your efforts. Look carefully at the items you got wrong. Were the items derived from the text, lecture, or supplementary materials? Bring your test to a learning specialist and have him or her help you determine your areas of weakness.

6.3 Do some preliminary studying for your next test. Generate a list of questions you would like to have clarified. Bring the list to a tutor or professor to seek answers.

6.4 Form a study group and create a mock test for one of your classes. Have each member pitch in a designated number of questions. Self-administer and grade the test you created.

REFERENCES

Alex, S. (1999). Note-taking shorthand. [Pamphlet]. Worcester, MA: Becker College.

Brown, H. (1996). Self evaluation of preparedness for tests and exams. [Pamphlet]. Boston, MA: Boston University.

Lister, R. (1993, February 21). Good study skills can and should be learned by everyone. *The Boston Globe,* p. 37.

Longman, D. G., & Atkinson, R. H. (1991). *College learning and study skills.* St. Paul, MN: West Publishing Company.

Myers, D. G. (1999). *Exploring Psychology* (4th ed.). New York: Worth Publishers.

Tuckman, B. (1965). Group development: Developmental sequence in small groups. *Psychological Bulletin,* 63(6), 384–399.

White, W., Mikulecky, B., Lake, R., & Ginn, M. (1986). Study groups [Pamphlet]. Boston, MA: Boston University.

Academic autobiography: your academic history, which includes your development as a student and the characterization of the type of student you were in elementary, middle, and high school.

Academic self-concept: the component of your self-concept that includes all of the thoughts and feelings that might affect and define you as a student.

Achievement motivation: Murray (1938) defines this as the "need to succeed" or the desire for significant accomplishment, for mastering skills or ideas, for control, and for rapidly attaining a high standard.

Active learners: individuals who believe that they are primarily responsible for their own learning, that they are agents in their own educational process.

Active reading: a general approach to textbook reading aimed at assisting students of all learning styles. The process involves utilizing multiple learning modalities: visually processing what you are reading, summarizing passages in your own words, and questioning yourself about your level of understanding.

Adjourning: according to Tuckman (1965) the last stage in group development, which involves establishing formal closure for a particular project, study group, or meeting.

American Psychological Association (APA) citation format: a system of accepted rules for formatting particular types of documents. The association publishes a handbook outlining the particulars of this system. These accepted standards allow members of particular professional communities to communicate more efficiently.

Annotating text: the process of writing analytical, critical, and/or summative notes in response to a written work. This activity involves writing comments, notes, and questions in the margins, essentially establishing a written conversation between reader and text.

Anxiety: the feeling of being tense, apprehensive, unsettled, and unsure why.

Attitude toward intelligence: Dweck and Leggett (1988) identify two implicit theories of intelligence: an entity view and an incremental view. People with an entity view believe that intelligence is a fixed, single ability. Thus, ability, not effort, is the key factor that determines performance. People who hold an incremental view believe that intelligence involves a set of skills that can be improved through effort.

Auditory learners: individuals who tend to favor their ears as the primary mode for learning. They are most likely to remember what they hear and what they say.

Automatic thinking: term used by Friedman and Lipshitz (1992) to describe remaining entrenched in old habits, in old ways of thinking and learning. They explain that students sometimes are immobilized to learn new information because of past experiences.

Banking model of education: Paulo Freire describes this educational model as one in which educators attempt to "dump" information into the minds of students via lecture and textbook reading.

Brainstorming: the process of letting ideas flow from your mind through your hand onto paper without making judgments as to how to say things perfectly, how to arrange the ideas, or whether or not you *really* want to include a particular idea. Brainstorming is about recording as much of what you are thinking as possible so that you can make these judgments later.

Campus resources: departments, people, and programs on college or university campuses that support students outside of the classroom.

Clustering: also referred to as branching, a process that involves a more visual approach to prewriting. Here, ideas are presented graphically as they relate to one another.

Comprehensive notes: complete notes with all levels of information, including generalizations, examples, explanations, transitions, questions, introductions, summaries, and repetitions.

Cornell system of note taking: a system of note taking that allows you to coordinate lecture notes with reading notes; an approach that involves, among other things, listing possible exam questions based on the notes gathered.

Daily schedule: a chronological record of how you intend to accomplish prioritized activities and/or tasks during specific hours on a particular day. Tasks and activities may be derived from your semester and weekly schedules, and/or from a to-do list.

Defense mechanisms: according to Sigmund Freud, ways in which individuals distort reality to reduce anxiety.

Delay gratification: to restrain impulses in order to put work first and then have fun.

Die-hard procrastinator: an individual who tends to get stuck in a rut to the point where he or she is completely immobilized.

Drafting: the process of turning less-than-cohesive thoughts into coherent phrases and paragraphs.

8–8–8 formula: for optimal balance with time management practices, the 24 hours in a day can be broken down into three components for college students: 8 hours for sleep, 8 hours for study, and 8 hours for leisure.

Emotional intelligence: Daniel Goleman's (1995) challenge to the way our culture quantifies intelligence. Emotional intelligence includes self-awareness, impulse control, persistence, and self-motivation.

End comments: forms of instructor feedback typically found at the end of a paper that are global in nature; comments that usually provide a summary of intertextual markings and marginal comments.

External locus of control: a generalized expectancy or feeling that outcomes are largely beyond our control and are a result of luck, fate, chance, or powerful others.

Feedback: the response you receive from instructors, learning assistance staff, or peer tutors regarding your academic work, studying, or behavior; a mechanism used to revise existing academic practices.

Feedback procedures: methods of discovering your level of understanding of a particular subject. The more common methods include predicting questions that might appear on exams, making summary sheets, tutoring other students, and self-testing.

Forming: according to Tuckman (1965) the initial stage in group development involving a group getting together to work toward a collective goal and determining members' strengths and weaknesses; the point at which the group discusses how to approach the task at hand.

Freewriting: a form of prewriting that includes the formulation of sentences and paragraphs instead of a list of ideas that would result from brainstorming.

Intellectual curiosity: defined by Peggy Maki (2002) as "the characteristic ability to question, challenge, look at an issue from multiple perspectives, seek more information before rushing to judgment, raise questions, deliberate, and craft well-reasoned arguments" (p. 6).

Intellectual discourse: a rational discussion about a particular subject with interested others.

Intellectual property: this property is unique in some way: it contains some new concept or data set, or perhaps argues against a previously established correlation. Intellectual property can be utilized by individuals other than the originator with permission.

Internal locus of control: a generalized expectancy or feeling of being reasonably in control over outcomes; attributing outcomes to your own hard work and effort.

Intertextual markings: these markings are placed within the text itself, that is, above, below, or covering your actual words.

Learning style: the pattern of personality and environmental factors related to how one learns.

Learning styles theory: addresses the ways in which a person learns best and tailors approaches to learning and studying based on the individual.

Locus of control: involves a generalized expectancy that people hold regarding the degree to which they control their fate.

Logic outline: an outline that includes a thesis statement—a sentence that reveals the purpose of the paper—as well as the points the writer will offer in support of that thesis—the supporting points.

Marginal comments: markings that occur in the (typically) one-inch margins surrounding text. These comments are usually a bit more global in scope than are intertextual markings, examining at least sentence meaning and often the significance of entire paragraphs.

Metacognition: strategies that allow students to plan, monitor, evaluate, and revise learning strategies whenever needed in studying and learning new materials; literally thinking about how you think.

Mixed modality learners: individuals who are able to function in more than one learning modality.

Modern Language Association (MLA) citation format: a system of accepted rules for formatting particular types of documents. The association publishes a handbook outlining the particulars of this system. These accepted standards allow members of particular professional communities to communicate more efficiently.

Norming: according to Tuckman (1965) the third stage in group development: when the group agrees on guiding principles or rules that each group member must abide by for the group to function most productively.

Office hours: scheduled times, typically posted on a course syllabus, when professors are in their offices so that students can meet with them to ask questions or discuss problems.

Paraphrasing: the practice of putting someone else's language into your own words, but still giving credit to the original author for her or his idea.

Passive learners: individuals consciously or unconsciously subscribing to the philosophy that others are responsible for teaching them what they need to know.

Peer review: the process of reviewing work with peers in a classroom setting.

Performing: according to Tuckman (1965) the fourth stage in group development, when the group performs effectively and productively—if it reaches this stage.

Plagiarism: the practice of presenting someone else's ideas as if they were your own.

Portfolios: collections of student work, with an emphasis on metacognition, requiring those who keep a portfolio to consider what it will include and how it will be organized.

Prewriting: the act of recording ideas with an emphasis on getting ideas in a form that you can see or hear. Prewriting is more about *what* you might say than *how* you might say it.

Procrastinate: to put off working on an activity because it seems too complex, difficult, time-consuming, or overwhelming.

Quoting: the practice of using quotation marks around exact words that you copy down from a source.

Rationalization: justifying undesirable behaviors with excuses.

Reciprocal determinism: according to Bandura (1986) the notion that there is an influential relationship between people and their environments.

Reflective journal: a collection of thoughts written down whose purpose is to help the author think through ideas by writing about them. The act of keeping a reflective journal involves making regular entries and collecting them together to illustrate thinking over a period of time.

Replacement activities: activities in which individuals typically engage other than those that should be priorities; activities that are typically engaged in during the process of procrastination.

Research: to investigate what others have said and/or written about topics of interest. Research can be done in many ways, including a search at a library or via the Internet, and by talking with experts in a relevant field.

Responsibility: this literally means your response-ability, that is, your ability to choose a response.

Revision: a writing process activity that involves carefully reviewing your work and making changes because a word, sentence, or paragraph in the writing interferes with the meaning(s) you are trying to convey to your audience. It is a good idea to look for grammatical and spelling errors when reviewing a piece of writing, but there are other things to look for as well. Of at least equal importance are unclear and/or underdeveloped ideas that could be interpreted by an audience in ways you don't intend.

Schema: a term used in the context of active reading. Schema refers to what you already know about the subjects that you find in your reading. Any new information presented will be interpreted/understood based on this prior knowledge.

Scholarly community: a group of people working toward intellectual pursuits.

Self-concept: our understanding of who we are, a conceptualization that encompasses all of our thoughts and feelings.

Self-efficacy: the belief that you are capable of producing desired results, such as mastering new skills and achieving personal goals.

Self-evaluate: to develop an understanding of your studying practices and procedures; to be sure that you did everything within your power to prepare adequately for a given test.

Self-regulate: to monitor your own learning and study procedures; a process under your control that is *your* primary responsibility.

Semester schedule: a schedule for an entire semester. A daily planner or electronic planner is used to record due dates for papers, projects, and presentations, and to enter midterm and final exam information next to the appropriate dates.

Storming: according to Tuckman (1965) the second stage in group development that occurs when conflict arises. The group must resolve these conflicts before proceeding to the next stage, norming.

Student-directed environment: a learning environment in which students are expected to adapt to the different demands of each class on their own.

Summarizing: an activity involving reducing a lengthy passage into a sentence or two while documenting the original source.

Switch cognitive gears: according to Louis and Sutton (1991) to transition from one mode of thought to another.

Syllabus: a document describing a course; outlining desired course outcomes, and detailing other relevant information, such as topics and readings.

Tactile/kinesthetic learners: individuals who prefer learning when they are physically involved in what they are studying. These learners want to act out a situation, create a product, or work on a project. They understand and remember best when they physically do something.

Teacher-directed environment: a learning environment in which teachers help students adapt to the different demands of each class.

Test preparation: all of the activities involved in preparing for an exam, including reading techniques, note-taking techniques, study techniques, class participation, and other contributory activities.

Theory of multiple intelligences (MI theory): Howard Gardner's (1983) idea that intelligence is not a single capacity that "equips" a person to deal with various situations. He argues that people use at least seven intelligences—linguistic, musical, logical–mathematical, spatial, bodily–kinesthetic, interpersonal, and intrapersonal—to approach problems and create products.

Three-tier time management system: consists of completing a semester schedule, weekly schedule, daily schedule, and to-do list.

Time management: a system for using time in an efficient and effective manner.

To-do list: a prioritized list of activities and/or tasks you need to accomplish based on your semester and weekly schedules. It enables you to meet the deadlines you've set for yourself.

Visual learners: individuals who use their eyes as the primary mode of learning. They want to see a picture; they want to actually see the words written down. These learners tune in to the physical environment.

Weekly schedule: a tool used to identify how much of your time is available for study. It is designed for writing in fixed commitments such as classes, labs, and job hours; listing times for eating, sleeping, grooming, transportation, leisure, and outside employment; then tentatively blocking out large spaces of time for studying.

Writing center: a resource on many college and university campuses designed to help students become better writers. In such a facility, a student can expect to work on a piece of writing in progress with a tutor on a one-on-one basis.

INDEX